YOUR
PILOT'S
LICENSE
4TH EDITION

JOE CHRISTY

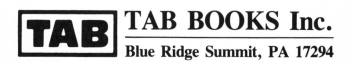

TAB BOOKS Inc.

Blue Ridge Summit, PA 17294

FOURTH EDITION

FIRST PRINTING

Library of Congress Cataloging in Publication Data

Christy, Joe.
    Your pilot's license / by Joe Christy. — 4th ed.
       p. cm.
      Previous ed. (1983) by Joe Christy & Clay Johnson.
      Includes index.
      ISBN 0-8306-2477-5 (pbk.)
      1. Airplanes—Piloting 2. Air pilots—United States—Licenses.
3. Private flying.   I. Title.
TL710.C475 1987
629.132′5217—dc19   87-19412
                                                            CIP

Questions regarding the content of this book
should be addressed to:

    Reader Inquiry Branch
    Editorial Department
    TAB BOOKS Inc.
    Blue Ridge Summit, PA 17294

Contents

Introduction

THIS BOOK is for prospective and beginning pilots. It is simple and informal, and it employs as many pictures as possible to take you through a typical civilian flight instruction course. The only thing I have taken for granted is that you know which is the front and which is the back of an airplane.

I try to explain all those little things that new flight students wonder about. I also explain the requirements, and do so in everyday language, with phrases perfected through years of experience in this field. I explain flight theory (without mathematics), basic air navigation, control-handling techniques, weather, air traffic rules, and aircraft instruments; and I offer a written exam for your private pilot certificate (with answers) which closely follows the real thing.

This book should save you time, money, and doubt. I believe it will prove to you that, if you are a reasonably normal human being, you can become a safe and competent pilot in a surprisingly short time, assuming that you approach this exciting new venture prepared to expend significant effort.

Pleased and proud that this book continues to be as popular as ever as it enters its 27th year of continuous publication, I have completely revised and updated this new fourth edition.

Happy landings!

Chapter 1

Instructors and Flight Schools

HOW MUCH do flying lessons cost? How tough is the physical exam? How do I get started? Do I have to sign up for the whole course, or can I quit if I don't like it?

Licensed pilots often hear such questions from their ground-bound acquaintances. Few can provide complete answers because their direct knowledge of the subject is limited to their own experiences. They might tell how they did it—which might or might not be the most practical approach for you—but it is unlikely that they can offer a current and comprehensive view of the entire flight instruction scene.

You might have more options than you think. It all depends on your age, your goal, and the amount of time, money, and effort you are willing to invest.

FLIGHT-TRAINING OPTIONS

At many small airports, particularly those away from metropolitan areas, you can still learn to fly the way it was usually done 50 years ago. You simply walk into the office and tell the flight operator that you want to start taking flying lessons. You pay for one hour of instruction at a time, phoning ahead to arrange for each lesson as your time, money, and inclination permit. While this might not be the best way to do it, for many it is the only way. Some people feel that it has certain advantages.

I did it that way back in the 1930s. Dual instruction (i.e., a plane with an instructor) cost $24 per hour, and solo time (i.e., plane rental only) cost $20 per hour in the Spartan, Travel Air, and Eaglerock biplanes that graced our little sod airport. During the Great Depression, teenagers were fortunate to find a part-time job that paid as much as $1 per day, so a lot of flying was taught a half-hour at a time.

Those conditions also fostered some "bootleg" flight time. A student could split the cost of an hour's solo time with a newly licensed (or, more properly, "certificated") private pilot and, for $10, receive an hour's "dual instruction" while the private pilot logged the hour as solo at half price. The Department of Commerce inspectors took a very dim view of such goings-on, and rightly so. It was a classic example of the blind leading the blind.

FBO Flight Schools

Today, the fixed-base operators (FBOs) associated with the major light aircraft manufacturers frequently offer a private pilot course as a complete package: flight training and ground school. Cessna dealers offer a time payment plan that allows you to pay for the course in eight installments over a year—or sooner, if you complete the course in less time.

Some FBOs, usually the larger ones, display a sign proclaiming that their flight training departments are FAA-approved. This means that the FAA has inspected and officially approved the facilities and curriculum offered. It is a guarantee of sorts, but it does not necessarily mean that the training offered by an unapproved operator is inadequate. Many excellent small operators do not regularly train enough students to justify the added expense of seeking FAA approval, while you might encounter flight instructors at FAA-approved schools who are not the best teachers.

Student instruction is seldom an FBO's main source of income. Aircraft maintenance, fuel sales, charter flights, aircraft sales, and hangar/tiedown fees normally account for the bulk of his business. Some of the small operators might not even have a full-time flight instructor on their payrolls. They simply put the student in touch with a free-lance instructor and rent the training airplane.

Don't expect a hard sell when you go to the airport seeking flight training. You might get the impression that no one wants to be bothered with people wandering in trying to spend money. Don't be discouraged. In my experience, FBOs are notoriously poor businessmen. Most would be much happier if they could just fly every day and not have to ask for money for their services.

Flying Clubs, Colleges, and the Military

In addition to the FBOs, there are several other routes you can take to obtain a pilot's license. Civilian flying clubs have been organized throughout the nation to lower the cost of pleasure flying for their members; many provide low-cost instruction, too. Many U.S. military bases have flying clubs, with resident instructors, but membership is limited to military personnel and civil service employees on the respective bases.

If you are still in high school and considering a career in civil aviation, the best way is through enrollment in a college or university offering professional aviation programs. These are two- or four-year courses, with academic credits accruing for the aviation subjects studied, including flight training. Two-year colleges award certificates or associate degrees, while four-year institutions award associate, bachelor, and even masters degrees. One advantage of the four-year schools is that your major doesn't necessarily have to be in an aviation discipline in order for you to learn to fly there.

A few colleges and universities, such as Embry-Riddle Aeronautical University (with campuses in Florida and Arizona) and Parks College (Illinois), are totally oriented to aviation. In these schools, all students are preparing for aviation careers.

For a more complete listing of college aviation programs, consult the *Aero Aviation College Directory* (TAB book No. 28907) or contact the University Aviation Association, P.O. Box 2321, Auburn, Alabama 36830.

And, of course, young people who can meet the high standards will not find any better flight training than in the U.S. Air Force and U.S. Navy. Because the training is usually in high-performance jets, this has long been the most certain way to the flight deck of a commercial airliner. A career in one of the military services has a lot to offer—to the right people—these days, including the opportunity to fly the most fantastic flying machines in the world.

There are several large privately operated flying schools and "academies" around the country, usually located at municipal airports and resembling FBOs in appearance, whose primary, often exclusive, activity is flight instruction. These schools are almost always FAA-approved and, therefore, have well-planned, fixed curricula, full-time instructors, provision for student residency, adequate classrooms, and modern training airplanes. They are, in a sense, aviation vo-tech schools. Most students at these schools are over 25 years of age—people who want to add flying to their other skills or who want to switch professions.

A private pilot's certificate has limitations. All of your flying must be done in accordance with the FAA's Visual Flight Rules (VFR). You need more experience and training to fly under Instrument Flight Rules (IFR), and you may not fly for compensation or hire.

The little dab of night flying instruction required for the private pilot certificate (three hours) is totally inadequate for safe night flight. In the beginning, you may skip the night flying altogether, if you wish, and your license will bear a notation limiting you to daylight flying.

GROUND STUDY OPTIONS

If you find it expedient or necessary to pay as you go, an hour at a time, you might also choose to study at home to acquire a thorough knowledge of the subjects that go along with your flight training: theory of flight, weather, air navigation, the Federal Aviation Regulations (FARs), etc. The Federal Aviation Administration (FAA) does not say how you must learn these things, only that you must. Also, you must achieve a passing score on an FAA written test covering these subjects. A recent survey indicates that almost 40 percent of today's licensed pilots received no formal classroom instruction in the required subjects.

Studying at home and scheduling flight lessons an hour at a time might not be the least expensive way to a private pilot certificate. You might need extra hours of flight instruction if you allow too much time to elapse between lessons, and it is certainly possible to pass the Private Pilot Written Test despite significant gaps in your practical knowledge of the subjects. At some later date, those gaps—if not filled in—could prove costly.

Knowledge is the key to air safety. You must thoroughly understand your flying machine and the several invisible forces that affect it in flight in order to develop consistently good piloting techniques. As obvious as that may sound, it escapes too many aspiring pilots.

I emphasize this point because more than 90 percent of aviation accidents are attributed to "pilot error," which I translate into "pilot ignorance." Poor decisions are rooted in inadequate knowledge.

The importance of the aviation subjects you study on the ground, therefore, cannot be overstated.

It is unlikely that you will gain your aviation knowledge all in one place. The slide shows and videos featured by most fixed-base operators in night classes are smooth, professionally produced presentations (often promoting a specific training airplane), but might be more effective at entertaining than teaching. I am not suggesting that you should pass up the chance at a formal ground-school course, only that you should augment it with some carefully selected reading at home. The audiovisual shows are not expensive and are monitored by FAA-licensed ground instructors (who are usually pilots). The ground instructor is there to answer questions and, if he does his job, will assign homework and conduct periodic tests.

COSTS

Flight training at FBOs, whether purchased an hour at a time or as a complete private pilot course, presently costs $30 to $40 per hour for the airplane and $15 to $20 per hour for the instructor. This varies a little, depending upon location and equipment, but assuming you are an average student, requiring 25 to 30 hours of dual instruction and 30 hours of solo practice to qualify for your private pilot certificate, you can expect to invest a minimum of $2,500 in the flight training. The ground-school course, books, and flight aids will add at least $200 to that.

You won't save much by seeking out an operator who has an old fabric-covered "taildragger" available as a trainer (Fig. 1-1).

Fig. 1-1. Instruction in a vintage taildragger may cost less, but it isn't likely to have the modern avionics that you should be learning to operate. Pictured is a Piper Super Cruiser.

It might rent for less money than modern tricycle-gear planes. And you might develop better landing and ground-operation techniques in it. (If your instructor scoffs at that statement, ask him how much time he has logged in tailwheel airplanes.) But it is unlikely that the old trainer will have all of the avionics (aviation radios) and instruments you must learn to use in today's air traffic system. Even if it does have the instruments, they won't be positioned in the standardized array found in the newer airplanes you will eventually fly. Most of your future flying is going to be in modern airplanes with the "tailwheel under the nose." You might as well begin with such a machine.

INSTRUCTORS

Flying and teaching are two different things—the former an acquired skill, the latter mostly an art. Select 100 flight instructors at random, and you will find most, if not all, are competent pilots. Perhaps 10 have outstanding ability as instructors. Approximately 20 possess almost no teaching ability, and the rest range in competence from barely adequate to good.

What makes a superior flight instructor? Patience, dedication, and experience—not necessarily experience in teaching (teachers are born, not made), but broad experience as a pilot. Many young commercial pilots on their way up have an impressive number of hours in their log books, most of that time straight-and-level, "by-the-numbers," and all in the same region of the country. Yet, some may never have spun an airplane or made an actual short-field landing.

You can learn to fly an airplane despite your instructor, but you might harbor some unanswered questions and have some knowledge gaps of which you are unaware. Or your instructor might be so inept as a teacher that you become discouraged and suspect that flying is something you could never master. It happens.

I strongly suspect that the occasional private pilot who decides to give up flying often does so because he was poorly instructed. He stuck it out and obtained his private pilot certificate because he is not a quitter. But for reasons unknown to him, he never became comfortable in the air. He fears airplanes. The fear is carefully concealed and is rooted in the subconscious belief that he is not totally in control of the aircraft.

An example of this situation surfaced during a recent conversation with a friend who happens to be an airline captain.

We were discussing aerobatics, and he surprised me when he said, "I almost quit flying before I got my private license."

"Run out of money?" I asked.

"No—out of confidence," he replied. "The thought of a stall made me extremely apprehensive—white knuckles, tight stomach, the whole bit." (Stalls are explained in Chapter 3.)

I waited for him to continue.

He shrugged. "I learned stall recovery during my dual instruction period just as everyone else does, and my instructor was satisfied with my performance. I soloed, and later, while building time for my certification ride, my instructor told me to practice a few stalls. It was torture. I knew that I couldn't continue with that anxiety, and I decided that maybe I just wasn't cut out to be a pilot."

"Then," he went on, "after that hour of practice was over, I was having a cold drink in the pilots' lounge when the old chief instructor came in and asked if I was having a problem. My expression must have shown my concern. I told him that I didn't like practicing stall recoveries.

" 'I watched you awhile today,' he said. 'Your technique is fine.'

" 'I always have the feeling that I'm just barely averting disaster,' I told him.

"The old guy had the remedy. He told my instructor he'd like to take a ride with me. Then he checked out a couple of parachutes and told me to fly us out to the practice area, attaining an altitude of 4000 feet. 'I want you to have the whole picture,' he said.

"Well, he wasn't talking about stall recovery. He took the controls, cut power, and brought the wheel all the way back. He held it into deep stall, gave it full rudder, and it whipped into a spin.

"A spin is something that really gets your attention, especially the first time. This gray-eagle-type did a couple, explaining recovery technique, then told me to climb back to 4000 and do one myself.

"You know, I ended up doing four of my own in that little Cessna. I was even beginning to enjoy it when he said that was enough."

"I can't speak for anyone else," he concluded, "but that did it for me. Stalls? Hell, I'd been two paydays beyond stalls! I had the whole picture. The unknown had become the known, and I knew I could handle it."

The spin ("tailspin," as it was known in times past) is, technically, an aerobatic maneuver, and can result from improper handling of the controls when the wing is in a stalled condition.

The FARs define aerobatic flight as any maneuver in which the nose of the airplane is raised or lowered more than 30 degrees, and/or the wings are banked in excess of 60 degrees (FAR 91.15); also, " . . . an intentional maneuver involving an abrupt change in an aircraft's attitude, an abnormal attitude, or abnormal acceleration, not necessary for normal flight" (FAR 91.71).

The FAA does not require spin training. Indeed, spins are prohibited in some training airplanes. And although I am aware of no polls on the subject, it seems to me that there are about as many flight instructors who favor spin training as those who claim that it has no practical value. Spin recovery was part of the presolo training prior to World War II and, of course, the military services have always taught it.

Most instructors, whatever their stand on spin training, agree that limited aerobatic training is desirable for students who plan careers as professional pilots. The advantages most often mentioned are increased precision and familiarity with (and safe recovery from) unusual aircraft attitudes. On the other hand, the essence of safety in the air is good judgment, and that means operating your machine within the limits of your ability. You can be a safe automobile driver without qualifying as a Hollywood stuntman.

Judging Your Instructor

But how, you ask, can you fairly judge the quality of your flight instructor, while recognizing that equally competent instructors differ in their perceptions of their obligations? While you should realize that your attitude toward learning is an equally important factor, here are some indicators of a good instructor:

1. It's not how much your instructor talks, but what he (or she) says that counts. Good teachers have the knack of dispensing with the superfluous and presenting a concept in the simplest and fewest words.
2. Your instructor will be keenly alert to your degree of understanding. If you do not thoroughly understand what he tells you, he will sense that and rephrase it as many times as necessary. He knows that a statement that is perfectly lucid to one person could be confusing to another. We all have preconceived beliefs that tend to hinder our grasp of some new subjects.

3. He will not overwhelm you with too many unfamiliar tasks or new concepts at one time.
4. A good flight instructor always explains, before each lesson, exactly what he wants you to do and how to do it. He will talk no more than is necessary during the flight (the noisy cabin of a training airplane is a lousy classroom), and he will discuss the flight with you after landing. Most of what he tells you will be contained in these very important preflight and postflight discussions. If you have a flight instructor who is too busy to conduct these sessions, get another instructor (Fig. 1-2).
5. A good instructor has a proven, well-planned syllabus and follows it.
6. A good instructor never pressures a student pilot, but relieves as much pressure as possible. He never hurries, shouts, or shows impatience. When a student repeatedly makes the same mistake, the instructor concludes that the fault lies with himself.
7. He knows that humor is a pressure-relief valve. That does not include horseplay or a cavalier attitude toward his

Fig. 1-2. If your flight instructor is too busy to conduct thorough preflight and postflight discussions with you, switch to an instructor who has more time. These sessions are important.

obligations, but the proclivity to laugh, rather than curse, at minor frustrations.

8. He is dependable. If your lesson is scheduled for 9 A.M., he will be ready at 9 A.M., and he will expect you to be 15 minutes early.

Mutual Respect

Your relationship with your flight instructor must be rooted in mutual respect. In many ways, the relationship will be as important as that which you should have with your doctor. Lack of respect from either of you is your signal to get another instructor.

You don't have to love your instructor. A good instructor is going to make as good a pilot of you as he possibly can, which means that he is going to demand as much effort from you as he can get. Depending upon your attitude, you could respect him for that, or you might regard him as an ogre. This need not conflict with point #6, above. He shouldn't pressure you, but simply stay with you and patiently upgrade goals as you progress. You will do yourself a disservice by looking for an instructor who will ask less of you.

Actually, you are not "taught." You *learn*. Your instructor cannot place a funnel in your ear and pour knowledge and skill into it. The most he can do is demonstrate, explain, and establish a series of attainable goals for you. The rest is up to you.

What about female flight instructors? Simple. I just said that mutual respect is necessary to a proper student-instructor relationship. The qualifications for a flight instructor certificate are the same for men and women.

This subject reminds me of a story that pioneer pilot and plane-builder Matty Laird likes to tell. During World War I, the Stinson sisters, Katherine and Marjorie, operated a flying school at San Antonio, Texas, where they taught Canadians to fly for Britain's Royal Flying Corps. When chided about their female instructors by U.S. Army Air Service cadets from nearby Kelly Field, the Canadians' stock rejoinder was, "So what? A woman taught me to walk."

AIRSICKNESS

Airsickness is usually explained as being related to the inner ear. In practice, however, student pilots seldom become airsick, and almost all of those who do soon adapt. A U.S. Air Force study revealed that 18 percent of Air Force student pilots experienced symptoms of motion sickness, but only 1.4 percent were eliminated from flight training because of it.

It seems that the controlling factor is apprehension or tenseness. Experienced pilots have been known to become airsick when riding as passengers. At the controls, pilots have other things to think about.

I am not saying that the aeromedical people are wrong about the inner ear connection—after all, Dramamine, one well-known airsickness remedy, appears to directly affect the inner ear. But the new and longer-lasting Transderm-Scop patch, although it is placed behind the ear, is believed to work on areas of the brain. So the brain also has an input (perhaps the dominant one). Ironically, it is a violation of the FARs for the pilot-in-command to take airsickness remedies because such remedies tend to induce drowsiness.

You should also know that it is unlawful to pilot an airplane while drinking any alcoholic beverage (or within eight hours of having done so), or while taking any prescription or non-prescription drug (or when suffering from any illness) that impairs a pilot's efficiency—and that includes the common cold. (See FAR 91.11 for details.)

Chapter 2
The Airplane

THE *lift* that an airplane needs to fly is produced primarily by its wings. Wings can be long or short, wide or narrow, but one thing they all have in common is *camber*. This is the term used to describe the curve of the cross section. Viewed from the side, the *airfoil* of a lightplane wing is shaped as shown in Fig. 2-1.

The deeper curve of the upper surface produces most of the lift. This is because, as the aircraft is pulled (or pushed) forward, air is forced to separate at the leading (front) edge and come together again at the trailing (rear) edge. The air flowing over the curved top surface has farther to travel in order to meet the air flowing under the bottom of the wing; therefore, the air above is forced to thin out and speed up. This produces an area of low pressure on top, into which the wing is constantly drawn in flight. Figure 2-2 shows how this air path would look if air were visible.

Lift is increased by tipping the leading edge of the wing upward, generating a deflection force from underneath to supplement the partial vacuum above (this also moves the partial vacuum or low-pressure area forward). However, the extent to which the wing may be tilted upward is limited—too much tilt and the flow over the top surface will be interrupted, eliminating the low pressure area and most of the lift. When that happens, the wing is *stalled*, and the airflow looks as shown in Fig. 2-3.

Fig. 2-1. Lightplane airfoil: The shape produces the lift. Pictured is the Cessna XMC, an experimental craft.

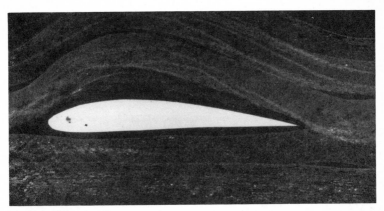

Fig. 2-2. Normal airflow pattern.

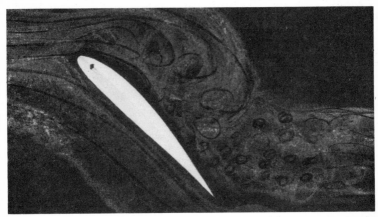

Fig. 2-3. Stall: The flow of air over the upper surface is interrupted, and the lifting force disappears.

13

ANGLE OF ATTACK

Everything an airplane does in flight depends upon the angle at which the leading edge of the wing meets the supporting sea of air; this is the wing's *angle of attack*. Angle of attack is the whole story of flight. The "wind" created by forward movement is *relative wind*. (Remember these terms; you'll be using them as long as you fly.)

The popular saying, "He lost flying speed and stalled," is misleading. Wings can be stalled at any speed, including your airplane's top speed. Simply increase the angle of attack past its critical point (normally 16 to 18 degrees in a lightplane), causing the relative wind to strike the wing well below the leading edge, and regardless of your speed, the air can no longer flow around the lifting surfaces in the smooth pattern necessary to produce lift. This condition can be induced with your airplane in any attitude relative to the ground: in a turn, a climb, a dive pullout, etc.

Actually, you have to work at it to stall a modern lightplane. In most situations caused by poor piloting techniques, the average lightplane will give plenty of warning prior to a stall, all the while resisting the mistreatment very determinedly.

CENTER OF GRAVITY

An airplane is a balanced machine that rotates three ways (on three axes) about its *center of gravity*. As shown in Fig. 2-4, these

Fig. 2-4. Axes: An airplane "rolls" about the longitudinal axis (Z), "pitches" about the horizontal axis (X), and "yaws" about the vertical axis (Y).

axes converge at the center of gravity, which is, in effect, the balance point of the airplane. To prevent an out-of-balance condition, there are limits to both the amount and placement of people, baggage, and fuel permitted within the airplane.

Not to be confused with the center of gravity, the *center of lift* is found in the low-pressure area above the wing.

THE FLIGHT CONTROL SYSTEM

The primary flight controls—the *control wheel* and *rudder pedals*—are connected to the movable surfaces on the wings and tail by steel cable or mechanical linkage. These controls function the same way on a lightplane as they do on a jet fighter or airliner (Fig. 2-5). By changing the camber of the wings and tail surfaces, they change the amount of lift generated by each of those areas.

Climbing and Descending

When you push the control wheel forward, the *elevators* (attached to the *horizontal stabilizer* on the tail) are lowered, pulling

Fig. 2-5. Flight control surfaces: A, ailerons; F, flaps, S, horizontal stabilizer; E, elevators; T, elevator trim; V, vertical stabilizer (or "fin"); R, rudder.

the airplane's tail up and pushing its nose down. Pull back and the elevators are raised, pushing the tail down and pulling the nose up.

Another way of thinking of the control wheel's effect is that forward and backward movement of the wheel, for the most part, controls your angle of attack; forward movement decreases the angle, and backward pressure increases it.

Trim

On some planes by adjusting the leading edge of the stabilizer up or down (with the little wheel mounted edgewise in the console just below the throttle), thus changing the stabilizer's angle of attack, the tail can be made to ride higher or lower to compensate for varying loads. This is called "trimming" the aircraft.

In the typical Cessna trainer, you achieve longitudinal trim by way of an elevator *trim tab* on the trailing edge of the right elevator. When the elevator trim is adjusted by the pilot, the elevators will ride slightly higher or lower, with the same effect as an adjustable stabilizer.

Some lightplanes have a *stabilator* in place of a horizontal stabilizer with hinged elevators. The one-piece stabilator reacts to the controls just as the elevators do, but a stabilator is more effective for its size than the stabilizer/elevator combination and allows a shorter fuselage with less airframe weight. Aircraft equipped with stabilators are trimmed exactly the same way.

In practice, the main purpose of adjusting trim is to eliminate the pilot's need to constantly apply control pressure to maintain a stable climb, cruise, or descent attitude. A properly trimmed aircraft will fly itself without control input from the pilot. But a change in power setting (such as that required to level off from a climb or begin a descent) will call for a change in trim.

Turns

Turning the wheel to the right or left banks the airplane in a corresponding direction. Turn the wheel to the right and you raise the *aileron* on the right (starboard) wing while simultaneously lowering the aileron on the left (port) wing. The airflow over the wings then forces down the right wing and lifts the left one.

Ailerons and rudder must be used together to produce a balanced, coordinated turn. If you press, say, your right rudder pedal while holding the wings level, the nose will point to the right, but you'll *skid* straight ahead. Similarly, if you bank to the right (or left) while holding the nose straight ahead with the rudder pedals, you will *slip*—tip on one wing and lose altitude—but you won't turn. So, coordinate rudder and ailerons to accomplish turns.

To establish a normal turn (about 30 degrees of bank), apply light control-wheel pressure in the direction of the turn, and return the wheel to neutral, except for a bit of back-pressure on the wheel to compensate for the G-force caused by your change of direction, and the fact that, in a turn, lift is not perpendicular to the force of gravity.

This G-force, which pushes you down in the seat during a turn, increases with the steepness of the turn. In a normal turn (30 degrees of bank or less), it is very slight. In a steeply banked turn, it is more pronounced. Because this force is pushing you and your airplane down, the wings must generate more lift to make up for it. Back-pressure on the wheel increases your angle of attack, providing this extra lift and preventing loss of altitude during the turn.

Wing Flaps

Wing flaps are hinged to the inboard trailing edges of the wings (Fig. 2-6). Although some people tend to think of them as "speed reducers," they are primarily "lift increasers." Wing flaps change the camber of the part of the wing to which they are attached, increasing the wing's lifting ability. For this reason, their use allows the airplane to approach for a landing at a much steeper angle.

Fig. 2-6. Extended flaps increase the wings' lifting ability.

Increased *drag* (wind resistance), a by-product of the extra lift, slows down the airplane. Also, the additional lift the flaps provide sometimes makes them useful for shortening takeoff runs on short or soft runways.

In the Cessna 150 trainer you'll meet in Chapter 3, you may use up to 20 degrees of flaps for takeoff. More than that would hinder rather than help a short-field takeoff run; in fact, the owner's manual advises against more than 20 degrees of flaps under *any* condition for takeoffs. (In crosswind takeoffs, the less flaps the better, and anytime you have plenty of runway available, it's best not to use flaps at all for takeoffs.) You may use a full 40 degrees of flaps for landings in this airplane, except in gusty conditions, when you'll want more speed and a flatter approach. Many pilots, especially while still learning, find a flatter approach with less flaps more comfortable.

THE PROPELLER AND ITS EFFECTS

In cross-section, a *propeller* is shaped like a wing. It produces "lift" just as a wing does, but in a different direction. Changing a propeller's *pitch* (the angle at which its blades strike the air) changes its angle of attack, which, in turn, changes the amount of "pull" it generates.

Most airplanes with engines of 150 horsepower or less have *fixed-pitch* propellers, because the lightplane's limited load capacity and narrow speed range cannot make efficient use of the more-expensive—in maintenance as well as initial cost—*constant-speed* or controllable-pitch propeller (Fig. 2-7). A constant-speed propeller turns at a constant RPM (revolutions per minute) setting selected by the pilot. This type of airscrew (as the British call a propeller) automatically adjusts its own pitch to compensate for the varying loads placed upon it.

Almost all propellers today are made of metal, though there are some laminated wooden ones found on homebuilts and restored antiques.

While on the ground, a propeller is dangerous. Never start your engine without *knowing* that no one is in front of, or approaching, your machine, and always call "Clear!" before turning the ignition key. Be especially watchful of friends who are unaccustomed to being around airplanes and their "invisible" spinning propellers. Wives, children, and dogs have walked into turning propellers they couldn't see. Pilots have, too.

Fig. 2-7. This propeller is the "fixed-pitch" type. The landing light, carburetor air scoop, and exhausts are also visible in this view.

Also, never trust a propeller at rest. A "short" in the switch system can easily furnish enough electrical current to start the engine if the propeller is turned by hand.

In the air, the propeller's motion generates several forces that tend to cause the airplane to turn. As air is dragged through the turning propeller blades, it is given a twisting motion. This *spiraling slipstream* of air exerts a sideways pressure on the left side of the fuselage (the central body of the plane) and vertical tail surfaces.

The propeller (which, in an American-made plane, turns clockwise from the pilot's perspective) also elicits a counterclockwise reaction from the engine and its mounting (Newton's Law of Equal and Opposite Force). These combined forces tend to rotate the entire airframe counterclockwise. At normal cruise, this *torque* effect is seldom noticed because the airplane is rigged to compensate for it (the engine might be canted slightly to one side or the vertical fin might be mounted off-center), but at higher or lower throttle settings, a little right rudder pressure usually is needed to maintain a straight course.

P-factor is the tendency of your airplane to swing its nose to the left in a climb. In a climbing attitude, the propeller's descending blade (the one on the right as viewed from the cockpit) has a greater angle of attack than the opposite, ascending blade. This gives the descending blade more effective thrust than the ascending blade, which causes the aircraft to *yaw* to the left in a climb. Again, correct with right rudder pressure.

THE THROTTLE

In modern lightplanes, the throttle is usually a big dark knob or a T-shaped handle at the bottom-center of your instrument panel. Pulled all the way out, it is at idle; pushed all the way in, it is "wide open." Its action is the same as the gas pedal in your car. In flight, however, it does not require the countless adjustments needed by its automobile counterpart. Normally, you set it only a few times for a cross-country flight: climb, cruise, and descent.

Basically, you should think of your throttle as your "up and down" control because, although backward movement of the wheel will point the nose upward, the engine must ultimately power your upward flight.

THE ENGINE

Airplanes have been powered by everything from steam to diesel (and, yes, plain ol' muscle-power). But as a private pilot, the only powerplants you are likely to encounter during the next few years are the air-cooled, four-cycle (*reciprocating*) gasoline engines similar, in principle, to those in automobiles. In fact, you may well fly an amateur-built (homebuilt) airplane fitted with a Ford 230-cubic-inch V-6 engine, or a converted Volkswagen "four-banger." Both Lycoming and Teledyne-Continental, leading aircraft engine makers, are currently trying to modify the Wankel rotary engine for light aircraft, and the latter is developing a liquid-cooled version of its 200-cubic-inch, 100-horsepower engine.

Unlike automobile engines, however, most light-aircraft engines have cylinders lying horizontally, approximately opposite one another, with the crankshaft in the center (Fig. 2-8). These are called *opposed-type* engines.

Electrical System

To achieve better combustion and greater dependability, each cylinder has two spark plugs. In fact, there are really two separate ignition systems.

Magnetos are used to supply ignition spark for the combustion chambers. A magneto is a generator, turned by means of a drive shaft driven from the engine. The faster the engine runs, the hotter

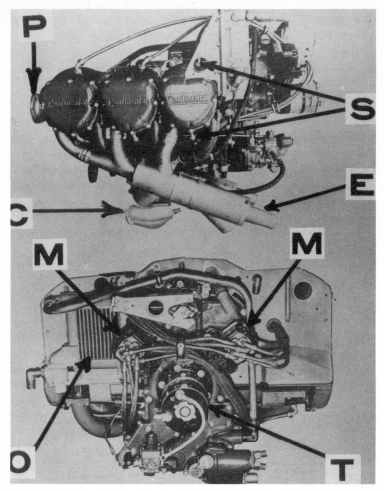

Fig. 2-8. This is a Continental six-cylinder, opposed-type, air-cooled engine: carburetor (C), exhaust (E), magnetos (M), oil cooler/radiator (O), propeller hub (P), spark plugs (S), starting motor (T).

the spark furnished by the magnetos. Because there are two ignition systems, there are two magnetos ("mags") controlled by a key-activated ignition switch in the cockpit. The switch has four positions: OFF, RIGHT, LEFT, and BOTH. The RIGHT and LEFT positions allow you to test each ignition system separately, although the engine is normally operated on BOTH. By turning the switch past the BOTH position, you engage the starter, just as you do in your car. Electricity is supplied to the starter and accessories by a storage battery in the engine compartment.

Primer

The engine *primer* is a push-pull knob located at the bottom left of the instrument panel in the Cessna. Its effect is much the same as the old manual choke on automobiles, except that it pumps raw fuel directly into the intake manifold rather than restricting air through the carburetor. Typically, one or two strokes of the primer are plenty for engine starting in warm weather, but you might need up to six strokes in cold weather (it varies with different engines). In extremely cold temperatures, you will need to continue priming while cranking the engine.

FLIGHT INSTRUMENTS

The basic flight instruments (Fig. 2-9) are the *airspeed indicator*, *altimeter*, and *turn coordinator* (or its predecessor, the *turn-and-slip indicator*). Most planes also contain an *artificial horizon*, *vertical-speed indicator* (VSI), and *directional gyro* (DG).

The airspeed indicator is a pressure instrument that measures the velocity of the air moving past the airplane. Actually, it is a barometer that registers the difference between the pressure of motionless air and the pressure resulting from the impact of oncoming air. To measure this impact pressure, a small tube facing the oncoming air is placed outside the propeller blast, usually in the left wing of single-engine airplanes. This tube is called the *pitot tube*, pronounced "pea-toe" (Fig. 2-10). (Like "pitot," many other aviation terms are of French origin: fuselage, nacelle, chandelle, aileron, empennage, etc. They originated prior to World War I, when France was more active than the United States in aircraft development.)

The airspeed indicator is not a speedometer, but merely shows the velocity of the air over the wings, the speed at which you are moving through the air. It does not take into account any movement of the air mass supporting you, the winds aloft, which can make your *ground speed* (speed over the earth's surface) very different from your airspeed.

The airspeed indicator doesn't even tell the whole truth about airspeed. Because it is a pressure instrument, varying air densities will cause it to indicate falsely. Air density decreases as altitude and temperature increase, so a correction must be made for these

Fig. 2-9. Instrument panel: This Cessna trainer is fully equipped for instrument flight. 1. Turn Coordinator; 2. Airspeed Indicator; 3. Directional Gyro; 4. Attitude Indicator (or "Artificial Horizon"); 5. Clock; 6. Vertical Speed Indicator (VSI); 7. Altimeter; 8. G-meter (for aerobatics); 9. VOR Course Indicator; 10. VOR Navigation and Communications Radios; 11. Automatic Direction Finder Radio (ADF); 12. Tachometer; 13. Fuel Gauges; 14. ADF Bearing Indicator; 15. Ammeter; 16. Suction Gauge (for the gyro instruments); 17. Oil Pressure and Oil Temperature Gauges; A. Parking Brake; B. Engine Primer; C. Ignition/Starter Switch; D. Master Switch; E. Brakes; F. Rudder Pedals; G. Map Case; H. Carburetor Heat; J. Fuel Mixture; K. Throttle; L. Elevator Trim Control; M. Microphone.

factors. These corrections can be obtained from a pocket computer, either the time-honored E6-B (a circular slide rule), or a new electronic version (Fig. 2-11). (Both types will also aid in the solution of cross-country navigation problems.)

Some airspeed indicators are equipped with a rotatable ring around the outer edge, calibrated to provide corrected true airspeed (with a little help from the altimeter and outside air temperature gauge). I'll explain how it works after I explain the altimeter.

The altimeter (Fig. 2-12) is another barometer, with its dial calibrated in feet. It works on the principle that air pressure steadily decreases with altitude. But, because heated air is less dense than cold air, to obtain an accurate reading, a correction must be made for temperature. Your pocket computer will speedily furnish the corrected figure.

Fig. 2-10. The pitot tube. Some are heated to prevent blockage by ice.

Natural atmospheric pressure changes often, so the altimeter must be set to compensate for local conditions. You can do this by turning a knob that rotates a small dial set in the altimeter's face. Before each flight, always set your altimeter to correspond with

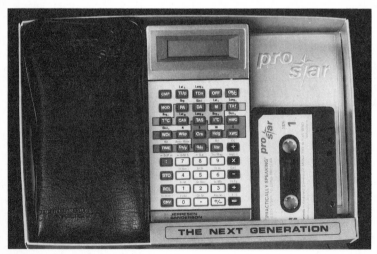

Fig. 2-11. The Jeppesen Sanderson Pro Star aviation computer, which performs every aviation problem imaginable, costs about $200.

24

Fig. 2-12. Your altimeter has three hands. The longest one indicates hundreds of feet; the middle one, thousands. The little hand registers in ten thousands. The altimeter at left is showing 2500 feet; the one at right, 6000 feet. These readings are above sea level.

the elevation of the field from which you are taking off. (This figure is usually found on a small sign beside the taxiway.) When you do this, the little window in the face of your altimeter will show the current sea level pressure. If this reading does not agree with the barometric pressure given by the control tower, there is an error in your instrument.

Remember that your altimeter always registers height above sea level, not above the ground. The altimeter setting given to you from the tower is the current local barometric pressure corrected to sea level. To maintain an accurate altitude during an extended flight, you will need to periodically adjust the altimeter to the current setting given by the nearest tower or Flight Service Station en route.

Now, back to the true airspeed indicator for a moment. To obtain true airspeed from this instrument, first make a note of the barometric pressure shown in the window of the altimeter so that you can return to it. Then change it to *standard atmosphere*, 29.92" Hg (inches of mercury). The altimeter needle is now pointing at your *pressure altitude*. Next, go to the true airspeed indicator, rotate the ring until the pressure altitude is aligned with the outside air temperature, then read true airspeed on the rotatable ring opposite the airspeed needle.

The vertical speed indicator is another barometer. As its name suggests, its dial is calibrated to tell you, in terms of feet per minute (FPM), how fast you are climbing or descending. There is a significant lag in the indications given by this instrument and, like the altimeter, it sometimes responds to a firm tap if it is slow to provide its indications.

The turn-and-slip indicator is really two instruments in one. The ball part looks and works like a carpenter's level, but with a ball, instead of a bubble, inside. It's your slip and skid indicator. As long as the ball remains centered, your maneuvers are well coordinated. The other part of this instrument, the needle, is controlled by a gyroscope, and it shows your rate of turn.

The newer "turn coordinator" provides the same information, but it has a little airplane in its face instead of a turn needle. The instrument is similar in appearance to the artificial horizon, but unlike the artificial horizon, it does not indicate pitch (up and down attitude).

The artificial horizon (or *attitude indicator*) is another gyro-scopically controlled instrument, and its job is to give you instant and accurate information as to your flight attitude in relation to the ground.

Unlike a *magnetic compass*, the directional gyro (DG) cannot sense specific directions by itself. You must first set it by referring to the magnetic compass, and it will then give you very accurate directional readings, unaffected by variation and deviation (two forces described in Chapter 6). Nor will it oscillate during a change of direction as does the magnetic compass. The DG allows you to hold a given heading and change headings easier and more precisely than by using the magnetic compass alone. But the DG does suffer from *precession*—it begins to drift off its setting after 20 minutes or so—and therefore must be periodically reset by reference to the magnetic compass (when the magnetic compass is steady).

All of your gyro instruments are driven by a vacuum pump that operates off the airplane's engine. Some installations have an electrical backup.

ENGINE INSTRUMENTS

Of the many engine gauges you might find on a specific aircraft, three are common to all lightplanes. The *tachometer* indicates the speed of the engine in terms of RPM. On lightplanes, tachometers are usually driven by a flexible shaft similar to an automobile speedometer cable; some are driven electrically. You adjust RPM with the throttle to achieve desired climb and cruise settings, to test the separate ignition systems, etc.

The *oil pressure* gauge is important because your airplane is dependent upon pressure lubrication. Upon starting your engine, this is the gauge you must watch. The indicator should move up into the color-coded safe operating range within the first half-minute of engine operation.

The *oil temperature* gauge serves your airplane as a water temperature gauge serves your car, by revealing cooling system malfunctions.

STALL WARNING DEVICES

Finally, all modern airplanes are equipped with stall warning devices. Cessna might have the best; almost nothing can go wrong with it. It's merely a reed—mounted behind a small opening in the leading edge of the wing—that starts whistling eerily at you when the relative wind drops below the leading edge of the wing and your angle of attack approaches the stalling point. Normally, it begins its warning about five or six seconds prior to full stall, giving you plenty of time to take corrective action (i.e., push the wheel forward). Other stall warners have horns that blow in the cockpit and red lights that flash on the instrument panel, activated by a sensor vane in the wing's leading edge. The biggest trouble with this type of stall warning is that the sensor might be accidentally bent, causing the warning to come too soon—or too late. The airplane itself, however, will warn you of an incipient stall if you're paying attention (as you'll find out in Chapter 3).

Chapter 3
Flying the Airplane:
Safely and Legally

MUCH HAS BEEN SAID about how safe (or dangerous) lightplanes are to fly, but you can sum it up in very few words: Airplanes are neither safe nor dangerous—pilots are. Like most other areas of human endeavor, it's what you make it.

Well, then, is flying as easy as the ads suggest? No, not if you intend to do more than circle the patch on nice days. Any reasonably normal person can learn to fly with eight or ten hours of competent dual instruction. This will not make you a professional pilot, but you'll be able to takeoff, fly, and land safely. From that point on, it all depends upon the standards you adopt. As in all areas of human accomplishment, the rewards and level of competence you attain are in proportion to the effort invested.

From the beginning, you should try to do two things in the airplane: think and relax.

An airplane is, in many ways, a very forgiving machine (the current buzzwords are "user friendly"). It *wants* to fly and, properly trimmed, will do so without help. But due to the lightplane's inherently stable characteristics, pilots who are too lazy to think fall into sloppy flying habits. They forget too soon their instructor's oft-repeated admonition: "You must always think ahead of your airplane." So, they goof off, and that can lead to trouble.

The problem is that you are seldom allowed the luxury of deferring a decision. Confronted with uncertain weather ahead or, perhaps, a dwindling fuel supply as darkness nears over unfamiliar terrain, you can't pull off and park while you decide what to do.

The solution is to have your options already planned. When decision-time comes, you must be ready. The guys and gals who have all those hairy adventures in airplanes are simply the poor planners—the non-thinkers. Their families are entitled to your compassion.

Your instructor will often tell you to relax. The physical sensations of flight are centered in your stomach muscles. During any change of direction, the forces acting upon the airplane, and you, will be most noticeable in your solar plexus. If these muscles are tense, their valuable assistance in helping you coordinate the controls smoothly will be lost. Also, tenseness brings on fatigue, and that dilutes both your judgment and your "feel" of your flying machine.

When you take over the controls for the first time, grip the wheel lightly; rest your feet lightly on the rudder pedals. Compared to the amount of force and movement of the wheel required to turn your car, much less is required to turn your airplane. The controls are sensitive and respond to light pressures.

So remember, always be alert, but not tense.

Now, let's go out to the flight line and become acquainted with our training airplane. We'll take this saucy little Cessna 150, the one on the end. She's beautiful, isn't she? How confidently poised is this sleek-winged machine! Properly handled in flight, she's as graceful as she looks.

(At present, you can expect to pay about $30 per hour for a Cessna 150 trainer, plus $17 per hour for your instructor. This will vary a little in different parts of the country. A lot of 150s are used for training because so many were built during their 20-year production run, which ended in 1978. The newer Cessna 152 is the same airframe fitted with an engine that has 15 additional horsepower. The 152 will probably cost you $35 per hour. The late-model Beech and Piper trainers are the Skipper and Tomahawk, respectively. These low-wing look-alikes are fitted with the same engine that is found in the Cessna 152 (and a lot of other two-placers). This engine, the Lycoming 0-235, is as reliable as more than 40 years' service can make it; the first one was fitted to a rag-wing Piper in 1940.)

Make a habit of observing your airplane as you approach it. If it isn't resting in a normal attitude, a landing gear strut might need attention. This machine has main landing gear legs of tubular steel that flex and take all the loads, and it has an air/oil shock strut on the nose wheel.

We'll begin with a familiarization flight. This airplane is two-place (carries up to two persons), weighs about 1000 pounds empty, and will carry about an additional 600 pounds (distributed between people, baggage, fuel, and whatever extra equipment you install). It will cruise between 110 and 117 MPH (95 to 100 *knots,* i.e., nautical miles per hour) using 75-percent power (depending upon altitude), and has a fuel capacity of 22.5 usable gallons out of a total of 26 gallons. That gives a normal range of about 400 miles, burning slightly over 5 gallons of fuel per hour.

PREFLIGHT CHECK

If you have spent any time around airports, watching different pilots prepare for that first flight of the day, you might have observed that some carefully and suspiciously inspect their aircraft before entering it to start the engine. Others do not.

Well, be advised, my fellow fliers, this is a quick way to tell the Old Pilots from the Bold Pilots (an ancient axiom holds that there are no Old Bold Pilots). There is no more important "maneuver" in flying than the preflight check.

So, let's start with the preflight check, sometimes called the "walk-around inspection" (Fig. 3-1). First we'll open the cabin door, make sure the battery and ignition switches are OFF, and remove the control-wheel lock. Next, we'll turn on the *master switch*—to the left there, below the ignition—long enough to read the fuel gauges (there's a separate gauge for each of the 13-gallon wing tanks) and extend the flaps. Then reach to the floor between the seats, and turn the fuel valve handle to the ON position.

Now, we'll walk around the airplane counterclockwise, starting at the tail and disconnecting the tail tie-down rope. Check for any possible damage to the tail control surfaces, especially underneath. Check for freedom of movement, and look carefully at the hinges. (I can recall a fatal accident that resulted when a pilot skipped his preflight inspection. A pen was found jammed in the elevator hinge of the wreckage.)

Continuing around the right side of the airplane, inspect the wing on this side. Check the aileron for freedom of movement, and look at the hinges. Check the right flap for proper extension, then proceed in front of the wing, disconnect the right tie-down, and give the right tire a visual inspection. Next, remove the cap, and look

Fig. 3-1. Preflight check. This common sense action separates the Old Pilots from the Bold Pilots.

into the fuel tank on this wing. Some high-wing airplanes have a convenient step for this chore; others require the use of a stepladder (Fig. 3-2).

This operation is much easier on low-wing aircraft, but the low-wingers have their disadvantages, too. In fact, there is a long list of advantages and disadvantages wherever the wings are placed—on top, on bottom, in the middle, or on each end.

We'll avoid that argument here. You'll hear all the pros and cons of each configuration in hangar sessions, and in the end, you must conclude that every airplane is a compromise, and that your choice is really a matter of personal preference (or prejudice).

Never trust the fuel gauges or the service crews. You must visually check each fuel tank. Although this might conflict with your natural tendency to be courteous to people (after all, the line boy is such a nice young fellow and he just said, "She's all ready to go, sir. Tanks full; oil okay."), just remind yourself that, if your

Fig. 3-2. Always visually check your fuel tanks. Be alert for the odor of jet fuel (kerosene).

engine quits on takeoff, or perhaps over mountainous country a half-hour from now, it won't be *his* neck that's in jeopardy. Also, your fuel gauges do not show quality, only quantity. Lightplanes have been mistakenly filled with jet fuel with sad results.

While you're above the wing, determine that the fuel tank vents are free of stoppage. "Mud dauber" wasps love to set up house-keeping there.

Now, be sure the gas cap is tight, and step down. Raise the cowl access door to check the oil, and pull out the fuel-strainer drain knob for about four seconds to check for any water or sediment (Fig. 3-3). Make sure that the strainer drain closes when you release the knob. If water is observed, it's possible that the wing tank sumps contain water; therefore, the wing tank drains and the fuel line drain should be opened for a further, precautionary check.

The most common way that water can get into your gasoline is from condensation in the tanks due to significant temperature changes overnight. Many pilots believe it is prudent to fill their tanks at the end of each day's flying, leaving no room for condensation.

Water also frequently accompanies the gasoline that's delivered by airport fuel trucks. So it's possible to find water in the fuel of the most carefully maintained aircraft.

After securing the cowl access door, proceed around the nose, and look over the propeller for nicks and dents. A nick in the

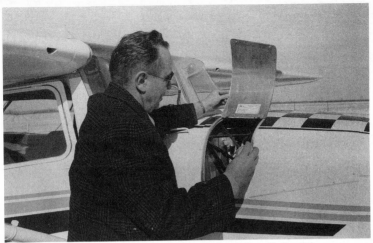

Fig. 3-3. Drain the fuel sediment trap and check the oil dipstick.

propeller's surface can become a stress point that progresses into complete failure in flight. The outer one-third of each blade (which produces most of the thrust) is the most sensitive to damage. If you are in doubt about a chewed-up leading edge or dents in a propeller's blades, ask an aircraft mechanic to look at it.

Next, check the nosewheel and nosewheel strut for proper inflation. Then, after visually checking the left fuel tank, continue around the left side, inspecting the left aileron and flap.

You're now back at your starting point at the cabin, but there are two more things to check on the left side: the *static air vent*, a little button-like opening on the side of the fuselage near the front, and the pitot tube, in the left wing. Make sure that these openings are free of obstructions, otherwise, your pressure instruments will malfunction.

Well, now you know more about your machine and have gained additional confidence in it. Let's get in (Figs. 3-4, 3-5). You'll sit in the pilot's seat on the left. Put your hand on the back of a seat to steady yourself; also, there's a boarding strap on the inside door post. Don't use the control wheel as a boarding handle.

Your seat slides on tracks just like an automobile seat; adjust it to suit you. Now, fasten your seat belt and shoulder harness. Comfortable? OK. Here are the things we'll do before we start the engine.

The parking brake should be set; check to see if it is. To set the parking brake, pull out the parking brake knob—it's the top

Fig. 3-4. Here's the interior of our training airplane, Cessna 150 Aerobat, Five Nine Three Seven Juliet.

Fig. 3-5. Comfortable? OK. The radio speaker is just above your head (R) and the boom mike is at "M," a practical setup for a training airplane. Later, you'll probably want your own headset. The flap position indicator is on the door post (F), and that's a boarding strap just below it (B). In the wing root is your outside air temperature gauge (T).

34

one there on the subpanel at the far left. It's marked. Now, push the *toe brakes,* hinged to the top of the rudder pedals, and then release the brake knob. Your toe brakes operate independently of one another, one for each main wheel.

Now look at your radios, and run your glance along the lower subpanel to make sure that all of the "electrics" are off. Then look to the floor to double-check that the *fuel selector* switch is still ON. All right, very good. You're ready to start your engine.

Set the *carburetor heat* knob at COLD. It's just above the trim wheel and to the left of your throttle, at the bottom-center of the instrument panel. The *mixture-control* knob is the red one immediately to the right of the throttle. Set it at RICH. The primer is the bottom knob on your extreme left below the parking brake; it's a warm morning, so give the engine only one or two squirts.

Now, lay your right forefinger along the throttle shaft with the throttle knob in the palm of your hand and your nail about one-fourth of an inch from the stop. Push in the throttle just that much (Fig. 3-6). Very little throttle is needed to start the engine.

Next, push in the master switch, the red button beneath the ignition key. That's good. Now open your window and call, "Clear!"

Fig. 3-6. Adjust the engine idle after start with your forefinger along the throttle shaft; note the RPM at far right. And yes, you sharp-eyed ones, we did switch to a different airplane for this photo to show you a transponder, which is installed just below your VOR Nav/Com radio. You must have a transponder these days, if your are going to go anywhere civilized.

Wait a moment and watch the propeller area to be sure it's clear.

Turn your ignition key to START, and as soon as the engine catches, release the key (just as you do in your car). The ignition switch will remain in the BOTH position.

She's idling a bit fast, so inch back the throttle, and slow her down a little. Watch the oil pressure gauge; as soon as its needle moves up out of the red zone, you're ready to taxi. Retract your flaps, and press your toe brakes to release the parking brake. (If the field has a control tower you will have to call Ground Control for taxi instructions.)

Applying a little power—it doesn't take much—start the airplane rolling straight ahead, and turn while the plane is in motion whenever possible. Turning from a standstill is hard on tires. By pressing one brake while releasing the other, it's possible to pivot very sharply when necessary.

For your first couple of flights, it's probably best, while taxiing, to keep your right hand on the throttle and your left one in your lap. Otherwise, you'll have a tendency to try to steer with the control wheel, but it won't turn you on the ground. Your nosewheel is linked with the rudder pedals; therefore, ground steering is done with your feet. During your second or third lesson, you will begin to use the control wheel during taxi because the flight controls can be useful for keeping the plane under control on the ground when there is significant wind (Fig. 3-7).

Operating from an uncontrolled airport, we proceed on a see-and-be-seen basis. The call I just made on the radio was a transmission "in the blind"—to no one in particular—on the UNICOM frequency in order to let any other planes in the area know what our intentions are. We'll use our radios more a little later.

As we roll down the taxiway toward the runway—hold 'er down there; don't go too fast—this is as good a time as any to elaborate on that carburetor heat control knob.

The throat of your carburetor is venturi-shaped (like a Coke bottle). The fuel/air mixture entering the carburetor throat is first compressed; then it expands rapidly, due to the suction in the intake manifold. Any gas, including plain air, gets very cold when rapidly expanded, and the suction through your carburetor can drop the air temperature as much as 40 degrees. Ice can form, therefore, in the carburetor throat when the outside air temperature is anywhere between 25 degrees and 70 degrees Fahrenheit. If this

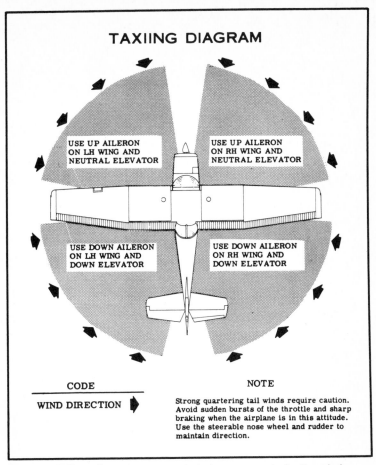

TAXIING DIAGRAM

USE UP AILERON ON LH WING AND NEUTRAL ELEVATOR

USE UP AILERON ON RH WING AND NEUTRAL ELEVATOR

USE DOWN AILERON ON LH WING AND DOWN ELEVATOR

USE DOWN AILERON ON RH WING AND DOWN ELEVATOR

CODE

WIND DIRECTION

NOTE

Strong quartering tail winds require caution. Avoid sudden bursts of the throttle and sharp braking when the airplane is in this attitude. Use the steerable nose wheel and rudder to maintain direction.

Fig. 3-7. While taxiing, use your controls to compensate for the wind.

happens, the fuel/air mixture to your engine is greatly reduced or blocked.

It shouldn't cause you any trouble because relative humidity must be rather high before this condition can occur, and because the signs of carburetor ice are easy to recognize. Your RPM will begin to drop; the engine will run rough and choke up. The carburetor heat knob is so handy that this condition need never become very far advanced.

Unless absolutely necessary, we'd rather not use carburetor heat for takeoff because it decreases the density of the fuel/air mixture through the engine and, therefore, subtracts some power.

The red mixture-control knob controls the amount of fuel metered into the intake manifold of the engine. This is desirable because, as we gain altitude and air density lessens, the fuel/air mixture entering the engine's cylinders will become too rich with fuel in proportion to air, if the imbalance is not corrected. The time-honored way to adjust mixture is to "lean it out" with the mixture-control knob in the cockpit until the engine begins to run slightly rough (too lean), and then enrich it just enough to smooth it out.

Well, you've given us a nice little ride down the taxiway. Gently apply your brakes, and come to a stop on the run-up pad, short of the runway, so we can run through the pre-takeoff check.

Had there been a tower here, the controller would have given us the barometric pressure along with taxi instructions, and we'd have used that to set our altimeter. But you'll note the little Burma Shave-type sign as you enter the taxiway on your next flight— what's that, you saw it? Good. It said 1390 feet? Very good; that's the field elevation here.

Turn the little knob below your altimeter to get that indication on the altimeter. Now you'll see that the little window in the face of the instrument shows the local barometric pressure to be 30.34″ Hg this morning. That's what the tower would have given us.

Because of the very warm temperature this morning, we've taxied with our doors open; now check that the doors and windows are latched—that's right, check mine, too. This is the pilot's responsibility, so you may as well get used to it.

Check your flight controls for complete freedom of movement. (You'll notice that there are pre-takeoff and landing checklists on a plastic card there on the glareshield. You should form the habit of referencing them prior to each takeoff and landing. They are short lists for this airplane, but they become a lot longer for more complex machines.)

Your elevator trim is that large black wheel set edgewise in the subpanel below the throttle; set its pointer at TAKEOFF (Fig. 3-8).

Holding the brakes, open your throttle to 1700 RPM, and turn the ignition switch to the R position while watching the tachometer. It shouldn't drop more than 75 RPM. Move the switch to BOTH again, and allow the other set of plugs to clear. As the RPM returns to 1700, switch to the L position to check that system. OK, very good. Return the switch to BOTH, and pull out the carburetor heat knob to make sure it is working. You should get another drop in RPM due to the decreased density of fuel/air reaching the engine.

Fig. 3-8. Adjust the elevator trim prior to takeoff.

Now, after a glance at the oil pressure, close the carburetor heat and reduce the throttle to idle.

Release your brakes, and carefully look for incoming aircraft. A good trick here is to swing the airplane in a complete circle so that you can get an unobstructed view of the entire *traffic pattern*. At a controlled field, you don't rely on your own eyeball scan; you go only when the tower gives you its blessing.

READY FOR TAKEOFF

No traffic? All right, you're ready to aviate. Roll into takeoff position and line up with the centerline of the runway. Smoothly push the throttle forward to the full-open position. Maintain a straight course with the rudder pedals (Fig. 3-9). She picks up speed rapidly.

After about 800 feet of ground run the airspeed indicator will sweep past 50 knots, and you'll realize that, in the meantime, the flight controls have come alive. Ease back on the wheel, and bring the wings to a slightly positive angle of attack . . . just a little more . . . there, you're airborne.

The nose is swinging a little to one side because you are not correcting for P-factor, so give her a little rudder to hold a straight course. In the future, you'll select a distant reference point to help you climb out in a straight line.

Adjust your climb with the control wheel to give you about 75 knots indicated airspeed (IAS). A shallower climb will bring your

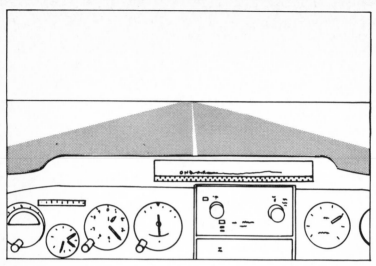

Fig. 3-9. Cleared for Takeoff: The throttle is at full power. Maintain a straight course with the rudder pedals.

airspeed up, and a steeper climb will slow you down. We select this speed and climb angle because it returns a reasonable climb rate, with good visibility over the nose, and doesn't tend to overheat the engine.

Leveling off, you'll adjust the throttle for cruising at 2500 RPM and tighten the friction lock on the throttle shaft to keep it from creeping. Then readjust your elevator trim so that the airplane will fly itself straight-and-level without help.

You'll quickly become accustomed to the effects of each of the controls, and it's best to put them out of your mind as you do. In other words, fly the airplane instead of the controls. Put a wing down, push the nose away, etc., rather than think of maneuvers in terms of control input.

I remember the reply a veteran pilot gave me many years ago when I asked him to resolve an argument concerning the exact handling of the controls through a certain maneuver. "Well," he said, "just do whatever is necessary to make it smooth and coordinated." At the time, I was disappointed with that answer; but later, I understood it when I caught myself holding opposite aileron to keep a turn rate constant. No one told me to do it, and I was unaware that I had been doing it. Unconsciously, I was simply doing "whatever was necessary" to make a good steep turn.

Control handling is difficult to explain because, like other skills

40

performed by "feel," your nervous system masters the technique quite independently of your conscious mind. You drive your automobile the same way, making countless corrections with the steering wheel and coordinating with brake and gas pedal without giving a conscious thought to any of them.

You might have a tendency to overcontrol your airplane at first, but don't worry about that because it is simply a habit from operating an automobile. You—that is, your nervous system—will soon become accustomed to the light, small pressures required for controlling your airplane.

As you enter a turn, rudder and aileron pressures are applied simultaneously (coordinated). Then, as the bank and rate-of-turn become established, the aileron and rudder are returned to neutral. If you continue to put pressure on the wheel and rudder pedal, the turn will continue to steepen (Figs. 3-10, 3-11). In steep turns, some opposite aileron will be needed, along with a little back pressure on the wheel, but don't forget that back pressure increases your angle of attack and, no matter how much speed you have, you can pull the wings into an unflyable angle of attack if you get the wheel back too far.

Another thing about steep turns is that as you tip your wings

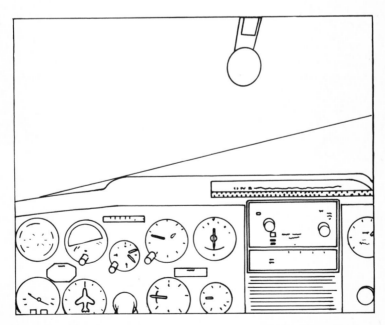

Fig. 3-10. Right turn: Rudder and aileron together make a balanced turn.

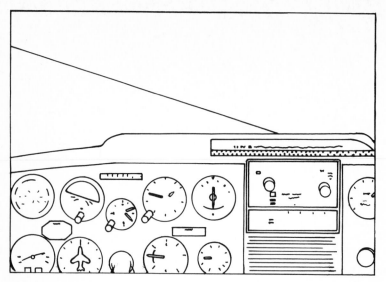

Fig. 3-11. Left turn: Return the controls to neutral after the bank and rate-of-turn are established.

sharply down on one end, their lift is no longer opposite the pull of gravity. The lift is still there, but it is at an angle to the force of gravity. In a 60° bank you are pulling two Gs, which means that your airplane, and you, weigh twice as much as normal. Military pilots have to live with the high G-forces generated by high-speed aerobatic maneuvers.

STALL RECOVERY

How do you know when you are about to stall? Most modern airplanes are equipped with stall warning indicators that light up, beep, or whistle at you. Our Cessna has a mournful whistle.

There are also natural signs. Controls loosen up, and there is a pronounced tail buffet as the stall is approached; plus, there is the airspeed indicator staring at you. The modern lightplane, however, is so designed that its stall habits are gentle and next-to-foolproof. In fact, this airplane's stall habits are so gentle, it might not be the best machine in which to demonstrate stalls. It doesn't want to break clean and fall out from under you the way heavier and faster airplanes do. Let's do a stall and see.

First, make a "clearing turn" to give us a good look around to make sure that our maneuvering isn't going to interfere with any other aircraft in the area. OK. Now, with the throttle cut back to idle, ease the wheel back and hold it there—that's right, all the way back (that stall warner is mean, isn't it?).

You'll note that the airspeed indicator has fallen clear back to about 43 knots—it's bouncing and hard to read. It isn't too accurate anyway in this attitude, because the relative wind is well below the leading edge of the wing and entering the pitot at an angle.

Meanwhile, you can see that the airplane doesn't want to do anything but mush along, bobbing its nose a little trying to find a flyable angle of attack. A glance at the altimeter and/or the vertical speed indicator, however, will reveal that we are losing altitude. We are no longer flying; the wing is stalled. But it is not completely stalled, and if you release back pressure on the wheel and feed in power again, we'll be flying again almost at once.

If you want to try the same thing with your flaps down, you'll find that there is a definite break, preceded by some buffeting, at approximately 38 knots IAS. The nose will fall through, in a determined effort by the airplane to counteract the way you are mishandling it.

Even more abrupt are the events that follow a stall out of a 30° (normal) bank. The buffeting prior to a full stall will be very pronounced, and the break will be quite clean, with the nose swinging earthward at a sharp angle.

Stop the yaw (turn) with rudder, get the wheel forward, apply power, and you're flying again. But the altimeter shows that we lost almost 400 feet of altitude in that one—which is why you can't afford to let these things happen when you are close to the ground, as on landing or takeoff. Low-altitude stalls, usually in the airport traffic pattern, are the single greatest cause of serious general-aviation accidents.

Except for practice, there is no reason why you should deliberately stall your airplane in flight, but we'll do more stalls later in your flight course to insure that you thoroughly understand both the symptoms and the remedy.

LANDING

Normal landing approaches can be made with power on or power off, with or without flaps. The determining factors in the kind of approach and landing you make will be, primarily, surface wind conditions, air turbulence, and the size and kind of airfield you are going into.

There are fewer gliding approaches and full-stall landings today than in the past, it seems to me, probably because there is plenty of paved runway for light aircraft almost everywhere. But it is still desirable to land on the first third of the runway and turn off onto a taxiway as soon as you reasonably can. You can overdo this, however. I wouldn't advise that you wear out tires and brakes, and impose heavy side-loads on the landing gear, smoking off the active runway at the first intersection at 40 knots. Like so much in flying, it's a matter of common sense, and the extreme course is seldom the correct one.

Plan your approach so that you enter the traffic pattern (Figs. 3-12, 3-13) at an altitude of 800 feet above the surface (that'll be about 2200 feet on our altimeter—for this field). Your normal descent with reduced RPM will then dissipate your remaining altitude during completion of the pattern.

Enter the pattern on the downwind leg about halfway or two-thirds of the way downfield, and at an angle of 45°, so that you won't interfere with aircraft taking off and so that you may best observe other traffic (Fig. 3-14). Return the mixture control to the "full rich" position (we had leaned it out as we gained altitude), apply carburetor heat before closing the throttle to idle, and establish your descent at about 65 knots with the flaps up.

"Play" your turn onto the base leg to compensate for weak or strong winds. The length of your final-approach leg will also be determined by wind velocity. If the wind is relatively strong, your landing pattern will be tighter. If the wind is light or calm, you will fly a longer downwind leg, your base leg will be farther from the runway, and your final approach will be longer.

We have a fairly long final approach, so wait until you turn onto final (Fig. 3-15) to lower your flaps. The flap handle is that flat one, shaped like a paddle, just to the right of the mixture control. It's an electric switch, so hold it down until you have the degrees of flaps you want—in this case, the full 40°. You can sure tell the difference, can't you? Get your wheel forward a bit more; we can come in pretty steep with full flaps without gaining any speed.

Pick out the spot on the runway where you expect to touch down, and watch it for a few seconds in relation to a fixed spot on your windshield (Fig. 3-16). If it appears to move upward in relation to your reference point on the windshield, you will undershoot your desired touchdown point. If it appears to move downward from your reference point, you'll overshoot your target. That's an ancient trick in making precision landings. Don't worry too much now about touching down exactly where you want to land.

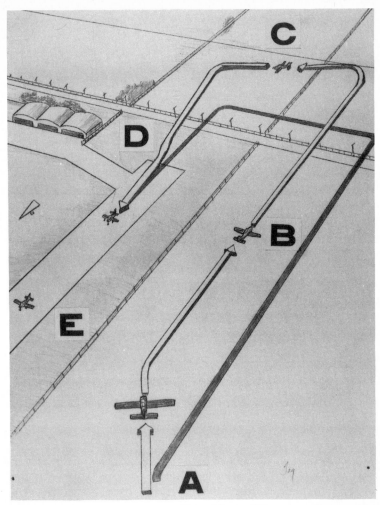

Fig. 3-12. Normal left-hand pattern: Enter (A) at a 45° angle so that you can observe other traffic. Lengths of the downwind leg (B) and base leg (C) are determined by wind conditions. Flare at D, holding the nosewheel off. Ease the nosewheel down as speed dissipates at E.

Greater precision will come with practice. For now, we have plenty of runway, and you are still learning the feel of the airplane.

Once you have throttled back and established a descent for your landing approach, you have also established the maximum distance you can travel before touching the ground without use of your engine. In other words, with your engine producing little or no

Fig. 3-13. Here it is for real: Entering the pattern at 800 to 1000 ft. above the surface and at a 45° angle to the downwind leg. The wind indicator is in the segmented circle in foreground.

Fig. 3-14. Downwind, parallel to the runway; your altitude is 800 ft. AGL.

Fig. 3-15. Turning from base leg to final approach. Base leg should be at least a quarter-mile from the runway threshold.

thrust, nothing you can do with the wheel and rudder pedals will add one inch to your glide. If you see that you are about to land short, your natural tendency is to pull back on the wheel to "stretch the glide." That will merely slow you down and cause you to sink faster. So, if you decide on final that you need a few more feet (or

Fig. 3-16. Final approach, and you're a bit too far to the left. There's no law that requires you to track exactly down the centerline, but precision might pay off someday.

a lot of feet, for that matter), open the throttle to get that distance.

Remember, you can pitch up the nose with the control wheel, but it's the engine that *powers* you up. In other words, the throttle is your basic up-and-down control.

If a landing approach goes sour for any reason, don't hesitate to open your throttle and go around for another try. Early recognition of the need to go around is important to ensure a safe margin of altitude and speed. The airport gang has a lot more respect for your good judgment in playing it safe, than they have for the vanity that sometimes prompts a pilot to attempt salvage of a bad approach.

Coming in over the end of the runway (Fig. 3-17), break your descent with back-pressure on the wheel at about 10 to 12 feet above the surface (this is the *flare*, or "round-out"). Hold the nose a little high, allowing the airplane to sink through the cushion of *ground effect* (the air is noticeably compressed between the surface and the wings below an altitude approximately equal to one-half of the aircraft's wingspan) and touch down on the two main wheels. Steer with the rudder—holding the wheel well back—and, as she loses speed, let the nosewheel come down (Fig. 3-18).

It's normally best to get the flaps up as you go forward with the control wheel to lower the nosewheel; both actions reduce lift and transfer the airplane's weight to the landing gear.

Allow the speed to drop as much as practicable before applying the brakes. Don't ride the brakes, and don't use them before the nosewheel is down. Now, clear the runway at the next intersection.

Fig. 3-17. That's better—not perfect, but acceptable for the time being. It takes practice. Begin your flare now.

Fig. 3-18. Rolling on the mains. Ease the nosewheel down, and allow speed to drop before using the brakes. Turn off of the runway at the next intersection. Never tie up a runway any longer than necessary.

LEGAL REQUIREMENTS

If, after your orientation ride, you decide to pursue a private pilot certificate, your instructor will refer you to a list of local medical doctors who are approved by the FAA to administer airmens' physical exams. There's a chance that your family doctor is on the list. The examination is not a tough one, but there are several conditions that could be disqualifying, including:

- uncorrected vision poorer than 20/50 in either or both eyes (corrected vision cannot be poorer than 20/30)
- colorblindness
- inability to hear a whisper at three feet
- mental disorders, alcoholism, or drug dependence
- epilepsy or other disorders causing seizures
- heart attack, angina, or coronary artery disease
- insulin-dependent diabetes
- any other condition that might prevent you from flying safely

Even if you have these or other conditions that could disqualify you (see FAR Part 67 for all of the details), you might be able to obtain a waiver, if you can show that you can safely perform your pilot duties.

If you have to wear glasses or contacts to pass the vision test, you will be required to wear them every time you fly as pilot-in-command.

49

Upon successful completion of the physical, the doctor will issue your *student pilot certificate* and *third-class medical certificate.* You must be at least 16 years old (14 years old for a glider or balloon). You must also be able to read, speak, and understand English, or else you'll have limitations put on the license.

The sole purpose of your student license is to allow you to fly alone after solo while building up the minimum flight time to qualify you to take the private pilot tests. You may not carry passengers with only a student license; your flying remains under the jurisdiction of your flight instructor.

You will be eligible for your private "ticket" after 40 hours flight time, but you'll probably have 10 or 12 additional hours before asking the FAA examiner to give you your test.

Private Pilot Qualifications

Here are excerpts from some of the FARs most pertinent to obtaining a private pilot certificate:

* *

FAR 61.103—To be eligible for a private pilot certificate, a person must——
   (a) be at least 17 years of age . . .;
   (b) be able to read, speak, and understand the English language, or have such operating limitations placed on his pilot certificate as are necessary for the safe operation of aircraft, to be removed when he shows that he can read, speak, and understand the English language;
   (c) hold at least a third-class medical certificate issued under Part 67 [of the FARs] . . .;
   (d) pass a written test on the subject areas on which instruction or home study is required by FAR 61.105;
   (e) pass an oral and flight test on procedures and maneuvers selected by an FAA inspector or examiner to determine the applicant's competency in the flight operations on which instruction is required by the flight proficiency provisions of FAR 61.107. . .

FAR 61.105—An applicant for a private pilot certificate must have logged ground instruction from an authorized instructor, or must present evidence showing that he has satisfactorily completed a course of instruction or home study in at least the following areas of aeronautical knowledge appropriate to the category of aircraft for which a rating is sought.

(a) Airplanes.

    (1) The Federal Aviation Regulations applicable to private pilot privileges, limitations, and flight operations, accident reporting requirements of the National Transportation Safety Board, and the use of the "Airman's Information Manual" and the FAA Advisory Circulars;

    (2) VFR navigation, using pilotage, dead reckoning, and radio aids;

    (3) The recognition of critical weather situations from the ground and in flight, and the procurement and use of aeronautical weather reports and forecasts; and

    (4) The safe and efficient operation of airplanes, including high density airport operations, collision avoidance precautions, and radio communications procedures.

FAR 61.107—The applicant for a private pilot certificate must have logged instruction from an authorized flight instructor in at least the following pilot operations. In addition, his logbook must contain an endorsement by an authorized flight instructor who has found him competent to perform each of those operations safely as a private pilot.

(a) In airplanes.

    (1) Preflight operations, including weight and balance determination, line inspection, and airplane servicing;

    (2) Airport and traffic pattern operations, including operations at controlled airports, radio communications, and collision avoidance precautions;

    (3) Flight maneuvering by reference to ground objects;

    (4) Flight at critically slow airspeeds, and the recognition of and recovery from imminent and full stalls entered from straight flight and from turns;

    (5) Normal and crosswind takeoffs and landings;

    (6) Control and maneuvering an airplane solely by reference to instruments, including descents and climbs, using radio aids or radar directives;

    (7) Cross-country flying, using pilotage, dead reckoning, and radio aids, including one two-hour flight;

    (8) Maximum performance takeoffs and landings;

(9) Night flying, including takeoffs, landings, and VFR navigation; and

(10) Emergency operations, including simulated aircraft and equipment malfunctions.

FAR 61.109—An applicant for a private pilot certificate with an airplane rating must have had at least a total of 40 hours of flight instruction and solo flight time which must include the following:

(a) Twenty hours of flight instruction from an authorized flight instructor, including at least—

(1) Three hours of cross-country;

(2) Three hours at night, including 10 takeoffs and landings for applicants seeking night flying privileges; and

(3) Three hours in airplanes in preparation for the private pilot flight test within 60 days prior to that test. An applicant who does not meet the night flying requirement . . . is issued a private pilot certificate bearing the limitation, "Night flying prohibited." This limitation may be removed if the holder of the certificate shows that he has met the requirements of paragraph (a)(2) of this section.

(b) Twenty hours of solo flight time, including at least—

(1) Ten hours in airplanes;

(2) Ten hours of cross-country flights, each flight with a landing at a point more than 50 nautical miles from the original departure point. One flight must be of at least 300 nautical miles with landings at a minimum of three points, one of which is at least 100 nautical miles from the original departure point; and

(3) Three solo takeoffs and landings to a full stop at an airport with an operating control tower.

* *

Staying Current

Although your private pilot certificate never expires, you are required to renew your medical certificate every 24 months. You must also undergo a *biennial flight review* with an instructor every 24 months, and if you want to carry passengers or fly at night, you'll need to meet the *recent flight experience* requirements of FAR 61.57.

Advanced Licenses

You will be eligible for a *commercial pilot certificate,* which will allow you to fly for pay, when you have a minimum of 250 hours logged. At this point in your flying career it's unlikely that any airline will hire you, so you'll probably "build time" instructing students and flying charter. There are separate tests for the *flight instructor certificate*, as well as for the *instrument rating*—the latter being necessary to all professional pilots except those who fly dusters and sprayers. The physical for the commercial license is a little tougher and comes due every 12 months. Also, the flight examiner will be more exacting in his check ride with you. The Commercial Pilot Written Test is chiefly concerned with navigation and weather recognition.

To be eligible for an *airline transport pilot certificate* you must be at least 23 years of age and possess a first-class medical certificate, the exam for which is, logically, more demanding than the physicals required for lesser pilot certificates. The first-class medical must be renewed every six months.

Ratings, which are special qualifications added to your pilot certificate (e.g., instrument, multi-engine, seaplane, glider), require separate tests.

Logbook

You are required to maintain a logbook of all flight time and instruction required to qualify for pilot certificates and ratings, including that necessary to keep your certificate(s) current. Instruction time logged must be properly endorsed by a certificated instructor, and student pilots must carry their logbooks along on all solo cross-country flights.

Legal Papers

Your airplane's registration and Certificate of Airworthiness must be kept in the aircraft at all times. The airworthiness certificate is maintained in force by way of an annual inspection of the airplane, performed by an FAA-licensed airframe and powerplant mechanic (A&P) with inspection authorization.

You must also carry your pilot and medical certificates whenever you act as a pilot-in-command or a required crewmember.

According to FAR 61.3, "Each person who holds a pilot certificate, flight instructor certificate, medical certificate, authorization, or license required by this part, shall present it for inspection upon the request of the Administrator, an authorized representative of the National Transportation Safety Board, or any federal, state, or local law enforcement officer."

That is the exact wording. It does not require that you surrender your certificate, only that you present it for inspection. No FAR allows a police officer to confiscate your airman's certificate under any circumstance. Only the FAA giveth and only the FAA can taketh away.

WEIGHT AND BALANCE

Flying "safely and legally" doesn't just mean having the proper training and licenses. It also means putting that training to work before every flight.

One of your most important preflight duties as pilot-in-command is to determine that the airplane is properly loaded. It's not much of a problem on our two-place trainer because people and fuel can't be placed outside the center of gravity (CG), and no baggage is carried on training flights. Soon, however, you'll be flying airplanes with more seats and with greater load-carrying capacity. Then, weight and balance becomes an important concern.

When you exceed an airplane's *maximum gross weight*, there is an increase in both stalling speed and landing speed. The aircraft's maximum rate of climb is reduced, and the additional time required to climb increases fuel consumption, along with the possibility of an overheated engine.

The aircraft's tolerance to G-forces is also affected. Assume that a plane has a load factor limit of 3.8 Gs. If the allowable gross weight is not exceeded, the wings will safely support 3.8 times the weight of the airplane and its contents. In "accelerated" flight (pull-ups, turns, turbulent air), the actual load on the wings will be much greater than the normal load, resulting in much greater stress on the wing structure. Overloading, therefore, has the effect of decreasing the G-load capability of the aircraft and might result in the wing being stressed to the point of popped rivets, permanent distortion, or complete structural failure.

The allowable *useful load* (i.e., passengers, baggage, fuel, and oil) must also be placed so that the airplane's CG remains within established limits. An airplane is in perfect balance when its weight is distributed in such a manner that it remains level when freely suspended. As long as the CG lies anywhere within the manufacturer's specified limits (or limits amended by an airplane mechanic with inspection authorization), balance can be maintained in flight.

Flight with the CG outside this range results in unsatisfactory or dangerous flight characteristics.

Due to the size of many baggage compartments, there might be a tendency to fill them to capacity, ignoring the placarded baggage weight limitations. This can throw the CG aft of allowable limits, creating a highly dangerous flight condition. The result would be a nose-high attitude that could lead to a stall from which recovery might not be possible due to inadequate elevator control.

Many owner's manuals provide shortcut methods of calculating an airplane's CG; you merely fill in some blanks with the load being taken aboard, figuring gasoline at 6 lbs./gal., oil at 7.5 lbs./gal., baggage weight, and passenger(s) weight, each total in its appropriate station.

Actually, if you know the *datum* position for the airplane—established by the manufacturer (unless amended by an IA) and found on the aircraft's weight-and-balance sheet—figuring the CG is rather simple. The rule is: Weight × *Arm* = Moment (Fig. 3-19). *Arm* is the distance from the datum, in inches, to the position of each bit of payload in the aircraft. The CG limits are given in inches, along with the other aircraft specifications, including empty and gross weights. Limitations and the empty weight of any given airplane may differ from those shown in the Owner's Manual if modifications have been made or equipment has been added to the original basic airplane.

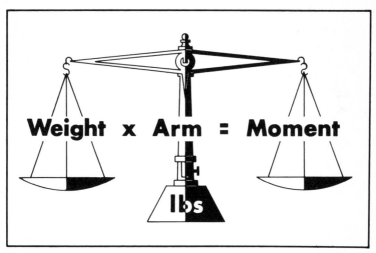

Fig. 3-19. Basic weight-and-balance formula.

Assuming a six-place Cessna 310, with CG limits given as 35 inches to 43.1 inches aft of the datum, aircraft empty weight of 3,450 lbs., and maximum allowable gross weight of 5,100 lbs., a sample problem could look like this:

Item	Weight (lbs)
Aircraft empty weight.........................	3,450
Pilot & passenger/co-pilot, 155 & 165 lbs...........	320
Two passengers, middle seats, 160 & 200 lbs........	360
One passenger, rear seat, 170 lbs.................	170
Baggage, nacelles...............................	200
Baggage, aft cabin.............................	160
Fuel, 130 gal..................................	780
Oil, 6 gal.....................................	45
Gross weight.................................	5,485

First off, we see that we are 385 lbs. over maximum gross weight. Some fuel or passengers or a little of each must be left behind. For the sake of the example here, let's say that we reduce the fuel load to 90 gallons, a reduction of 240 lbs. and eliminate 145 lbs. of baggage from the nacelles. That brings us down to the maximum legal load.

Now, we'll determine whether or not the load is distributed so that the CG limits are not violated. Using the arms given in the owner's manual, and the weights calculated above, we obtain the following:

Item	Weight (lbs)	× Arm (in.)	= Moment (lb-in.)
Aircraft empty weight	3,450	36.5	125,925.0
Pilot & Co-pilot	320	37.0	11,840.0
Two passengers (middle)	360	71.7	25,812.0
One passenger (rear)	170	105.0	17,850.0
Baggage (nacelles)	55	63.0	3,465.0
Baggage (aft cabin)	160	124.0	19,840.0
Fuel (90 gal.)	540	35.0	18,900.0
Oil (6 gal.)	45	3.5	157.5
Total	5,100		223,789.5

$$\text{Center of Gravity} = \frac{\text{Total Moment}}{\text{Total Weight}} = \frac{223,789.5}{5,100} = 43.88 \text{ (in.)}$$

Out of limits again. We are .78 inch behind the aft limit of 43.1 in. Some of the load will have to be moved forward. Let's shift 145 lbs of the baggage from the aft cabin to the nacelles.

Item	Weight (lbs.) ×	Arm (in.)	=	Moment (lb-in.)
Baggage (nacelles)	200	63.0		12,600.0
Baggage (aft cabin)	15	124.0		1,860.0

Using these new moments, we discover that the total moment has changed to 214,944.5. Total weight, of course, remains the same: 5,100 lbs.

$$\text{Center of Gravity} = \frac{214,944.5}{5,100} = 42.15 \text{ (in.)}$$

Now it's within limits. There are, however, two more things we should normally investigate: the effect of fuel burn on the CG, and a determination as to whether or not we have enough fuel, plus reserves, for the trip planned. The latter consideration is influenced by forecast winds.

Chapter 4
Control Techniques

EXPERIENCED FLIGHT INSTRUCTORS usually try to avoid word-iness in the explanations they give to student pilots. After explaining the same things hundreds of times to hundreds of different people—and noting that certain short phrases seem to most often turn on the light of understanding—they acquire a small collection of favorite sayings, "words to fly by," so to speak. You will hear them often, and your instructor expects you to forever store them in a convenient place in your mind for instant and useful recall.

That is as it should be; these pregnant little sayings contain as much truth as is possible to pack into a few words. But you must accept them for what they are: *reminders* of the basics. Most will contain implications beyond the basic truth offered.

For example, I said earlier that angle of attack is the whole story of flight. Well, that's true, but it assumes that your engine is functioning properly.

Instructors seldom describe maneuvers in terms of angle of attack, presumably because air is invisible and pilots can't see its flow around the wing. But they make oblique reference to it very often when they mention the pitch attitude of your aircraft.

One of the neat little sayings you will hear so often as a student pilot is "Pitch plus power equals performance." This is totally accurate, yet it too, requires some elaboration because, within limits, performance values are interchangeable. You can make trade-offs among altitude, airspeed, and range.

Let's do a simple experiment in our training airplane to demonstrate this concept.

You are trimmed for straight-and-level flight, cruising at approximately 65-percent power. Now, without moving the flight controls, increase power. Do you speed up? No. You begin to climb.

Why didn't you simply gain airspeed? You were straight and level; you didn't pull back the wheel to raise the nose.

Well, had you wanted to increase airspeed it would have been necessary to decrease the angle of attack along with the increase in power. You see, straight and level, using 65 percent of the available power, you had the airplane trimmed to whatever angle of attack was required to exactly balance lift against gravity. Additional power meant added lift at that angle of attack. Depending upon altitude (air density), you could have also climbed by applying back-pressure on the control wheel, in which case you would have done so at the expense of airspeed. You could have remained straight and level, while increasing airspeed, by applying forward pressure on the control wheel, and then retrimming to fly at the decreased angle of attack.

This is what is meant by the "limited interchangeability" of altitude and airspeed. It is limited because unless you add more power, such a trade-off requires that you *have* excess airspeed to be traded.

In practice, you will normally make minor altitude corrections with pitch—with back pressure or forward pressure on the control wheel—because the airspeed changes are relatively insignificant. And learning to fly instruments, you will be told to control altitude with pitch and airspeed with power.

Pitch and power are interdependent. Unless you fully understand this interdependence, aircraft control might be confusing in the beginning.

LOAD AND AIR DENSITY

To safely control your airplane, you must understand two important factors that influence your airplane's performance: the load it is carrying and the density of the air.

Given the same amount of thrust/power, a heavily loaded airplane must fly at a greater angle of attack than a lightly loaded machine. Although an increase in power (if possible) will compensate for a heavier load, normally a fully loaded airplane is simply trimmed to fly at an increased angle of attack and pays the cost in airspeed. It will also stall at a higher airspeed.

Air density affects aircraft performance in two ways. As the atmosphere thins out with altitude and/or heat (and humidity), an engine loses power—and wings produce less lift.

An engine loses power as you climb to higher altitudes because the volume of fuel/air mixture through the carburetor is steadily reduced. At somewhere around 7500 feet above sea level, lightplane engines (without superchargers) produce about 75 percent of their rated horsepower at full throttle, and output diminishes markedly after that. By the time a plane like our trainer has struggled to 14,000 feet (its *service ceiling*), its rate-of-climb has eroded to a tentative 100 feet per minute. Shortly after takeoff it was giving us more than 600 feet per minute.

Some four- and six-place lightplanes are available with *superchargers*. A supercharger is a gear-driven air pump that packs more fuel/air mixture into the intake manifold, allowing your engine to develop its rated power (or a high percentage of it) to a much higher altitude than is possible with a normally aspirated engine. The superchargers found on American light aircraft are usually referred to as *turbochargers*, because they compress air by means of a small turbine driven by the engine's exhaust.

Temperature also affects air density. Warm air is thinner than cold air, and that can make a great deal of difference to pilots. Several years ago, I watched with concealed amusement as a 225-pound pilot tried in vain to take off at Albuquerque in a 65-HP Piper Cub on a hot day. The airport there is about 5000 feet above sea level, and a temperature in the high 90s added the equivalent of another two or three thousand (a low barometer could add even more). The Cub's engine was probably producing no more than 45 HP at that *density altitude*. At the same time, its wings needed to be propelled down the runway at a much greater velocity than would have been required in denser air.

After three attempts, the pilot gave up. Even if he had managed to become airborne, his climb rate would have been near zero, and he probably could not have climbed above the ground effect.

Pilots who fly from high-altitude airfields in the West are more acutely aware of density altitude problems than "flatlanders," but, even at the lower elevations, air temperature can make a great deal of difference in takeoff and landing requirements, as well as in climb performance.

It is easy to obtain an accurate estimate of the additional take-off run required on warm days by referencing the graphs or charts in your airplane owner's manual, or by use of an electronic aviation pocket computer.

An airplane, at any given gross weight, will always require the same quantity of air molecules flowing around its wings to support that weight. That means more *true* airspeed (TAS) is needed in thin air than in heavy air. *Indicated* airspeed, however, remains the same. That's because you must move faster through thin air to impact enough air molecules to obtain the same reading that would register at a lower true airspeed in denser air. Remember, the airspeed indicator is a pressure instrument.

In other words, if your airplane stalls at 55 kts. *indicated* when fully loaded, it will *always* stall at 55 kts. *indicated*, whatever the altitude and/or temperature—although the TAS will vary.

The only thing that matters to your wing is that a sufficient quantity of air molecules flow around it at a flyable angle of attack.

TAKEOFFS, CLIMBS, AND DESCENTS

On takeoff, a headwind allows an airplane to reach liftoff speed at a lower ground speed than in a no-wind condition, while a tailwind forces it to achieve a greater ground speed to attain liftoff speed. In both cases, however, the airspeed (the speed the plane feels) at liftoff is the same.

A headwind that is 10 percent of the takeoff airspeed will reduce the takeoff distance approximately 19 percent, and a headwind of 50 percent of takeoff speed will reduce takeoff distance by 75 percent. A tailwind that is 10 percent of the takeoff airspeed will increase the takeoff distance approximately 21 percent.

To estimate takeoff distance, use the airplane's operating manual to adjust for the following variables:

- Pressure altitude and temperature—to determine the density altitude and its affect.
- Gross weight—has a large effect on takeoff distance.
- Runway slope and condition—the effect of an incline, retarding effect of snow, ice, etc.
- Wind—large effect on takeoff distance.

The most adverse conditions for takeoff performance are the result of a combination of high gross weight, high altitude, high temperature, and unfavorable wind. The effect of wind on landing distance is identical to the effect on takeoff distance.

Quite early in your training you will be introduced to your airplane's various climb gaits. The usual procedure is to select the power setting for the kind of climb desired, then adjust the airspeed with pitch. With the airplane trimmed for climb, for a given amount of thrust, there is an angle of attack that will give you the most altitude possible in the shortest distance: *best angle-of-climb*. There is also an angle of attack that will give you the *best rate-of-climb* in terms of feet per minute, and there are thrust-pitch combinations that favor airspeed over climb rate in order to get you to your destination faster. The point is, with climb power applied, you determine climb rate with pitch (angle of attack), while referencing your airspeed indicator.

A given power setting and airspeed, with the airplane trimmed for climb, will seldom return exactly the same rate-of-climb on each flight, because air density and aircraft load are variables. Therefore, while the airplane's operating manual will tell you that a certain RPM setting and airspeed will provide, say, the best rate-of-climb, that rate (the actual number of feet per minute) will vary some.

As with other maneuvers, climbs should be performed by using both flight instruments and outside visual references. The normal climb speed given in the airplane's operating manual should be used in most cases. This is usually very close to the airplane's best rate-of-climb airspeed, but may be slightly higher to give better engine cooling and/or better visibility over the nose.

The effects of torque at the climb power setting are a primary factor in climbs. Because the climb airspeed is lower than cruising speed, the airplane's angle of attack is relatively high. With these conditions, torque and asymmetrical loading of the propeller (P-factor) cause the airplane to have a tendency to roll and yaw to the left. To counteract this, right rudder pressure must be used.

Trim is also important during a climb. After the climbing attitude, power setting, and airspeed have been established, the airplane should be trimmed to relieve all pressures on the controls.

In summary, you establish your climb by adjusting the RPM with the throttle to whatever power setting is recommended, then you apply back elevator pressure to adjust the recommended airspeed with pitch. Correct for torque with rudder pressure, and then trim away the pressures on the control wheel.

As the airplane gains altitude during a climb, the *manifold pressure* gauge (if the airplane is so equipped) will show a loss of pressure, because the air entering the engine's induction system gradually decreases in density as altitude increases. This will occur at the rate of approximately 1″ Hg of manifold pressure for each 1000 feet. During prolonged climbs, then, the throttle must be continually advanced if constant power is to be maintained.

You will start to level off approximately 50 feet below your desired altitude by lowering the nose to the level-flight attitude. Do it gradually, because you will actually lose altitude if you lower the nose to level flight without allowing the airspeed to build proportionately. As you lower the nose, retrim the airplane.

Maintain climb power temporarily after you achieve a level attitude so that you will accelerate to the desired cruising airspeed. When you reach your desired cruising speed (or slightly above it), back off the throttle to the cruise power setting you want, adjust the mixture control to a lean position, and retrim the airplane for "hands off" flight.

As for descending flight, power-off descents (glides) are like power-off landing approaches, and it is necessary that they be performed more subconsciously than other maneuvers because most of the time in a descent you will be giving full attention to details other than the handling of the controls.

The manufacturer usually lists the airplane's optimum gliding speed. If you don't have it, you may discover it for yourself by establishing a power-off glide and noting the airspeed and rate of descent on the vertical-speed indicator (give the VSI time to stabilize), then gradually reduce the airspeed with pitch until the rate of descent reaches its minimum and starts to increase. This is your best glide speed in still air, that is, the airspeed and pitch attitude that will take you forward the maximum number of feet for each foot of altitude lost. With the glide established, trim away the control pressures.

Because of the airplane's inertia, you need to start to level off from a glide 100 to 150 feet before reaching the desired altitude. At the same time, add power for the appropriate level-flight cruise setting so that the desired airspeed will be reached as you finish leveling off.

TURNS

As mentioned in Chapter 2, turns are accomplished by lowering the wing in the direction of the desired turn, and simultaneously applying rudder pressure in the same direction. The bank causes the turn, while the proper amount of rudder prevents the airplane from skidding to the outside of the turn or slipping to the inside of the turn. For this reason, some instructors tell their students to think of the rudder as a trimming device. Also, the use of rudder counters *adverse yaw,* which is the tendency of the airplane's nose to swing opposite to the direction of the turn because of the increased drag produced by the raised wing, which must speed up because it is on the outside of the turn. A contributing factor is that the down-aileron on the raised wing creates more drag than does the up-aileron on the lowered wing.

Turns can be divided into three classes: shallow, medium, and steep. *Shallow turns* are those in which the bank is less than approximately 20° and require that some control pressure be held to maintain the bank, because the airplane's inherent stability tends to level the wings. This stability around the airplane's longitudinal axis is due to *dihedral,* the slight degree to which each wing is angled upward from root to tip.

Medium turns are those resulting from a degree of bank (approximately 20-45°) at which the airplane tends to hold a constant bank with no control force on the ailerons. Most instructors introduce students to medium-banked turns first, turns of about 30° of bank.

Steep turns are those in which the bank exceeds 45° and the airplane's "overbanking" tendency shows up. That is, the bank tends to increase unless opposite aileron is applied to overcome it.

Now, let's examine a medium-banked turn in detail. The turn should be started by gradually and simultaneously applying pressure in the desired direction to both the aileron and rudder. The rate at which the airplane rolls into the turn is governed by the rapidity and amount of control pressures applied, so be smooth.

As the airplane rolls about its longitudinal axis upon entering the turn, increase your pitch attitude. In all turns in which a constant altitude is to be maintained, it is necessary to increase the angle of attack by applying back elevator pressure. This is necessary because part of the lift that you were using to maintain straight-and-level flight is now being used to turn the airplane and overcome centrifugal force.

The amount of back pressure needed will be negligible to nonexistent in shallow turns, and very pronounced in steep turns. But you know that pitch and power are always tied together, so you may substitute one for the other to a limited extent. A significant change in either, however, demands a compensating adjustment in the other. Ignore that basic truth and you will pay the price in either airspeed or altitude.

During very steep turns, in addition to back pressure, you might even need to add power to maintain a safe airspeed. Frequently, there is a tendency for the airplane's nose to lower, resulting in a loss of altitude.

(To recover from an unintentional nose-low attitude during a steep turn, you should first reduce the angle of bank with coordinated aileron and rudder pressure. Then, apply back elevator pressure to raise the airplane's nose to the desired pitch attitude. After that, reestablish the desired angle of bank. Do not attempt to raise the nose *before* reducing the angle of bank, because that will just tighten the descending spiral and could lead to overstressing the airplane.)

As soon as the airplane rolls from the wings-level attitude, the nose should also start to move along the horizon, increasing its rate of travel proportionately as the bank is increased. Any variation from this is indicative of a specific control being misused:

- If the nose starts to move before the bank starts, rudder is being applied too soon.
- If the bank starts before the nose starts turning, or if the nose moves in the opposite direction, the rudder is being used too late.
- If the nose moves up or down when entering the bank, excessive or insufficient back elevator pressure is being applied.

As the desired angle of bank is established, relax the pressures on the aileron and rudder, allowing them to streamline in their neutral positions. The back elevator pressure should *not* be released but, rather, held constant or sometimes increased to maintain a constant altitude.

Throughout the turn, cross-check your references on the horizon and occasionally include the altimeter to determine whether or not your pitch attitude is correct. If gaining or losing altitude, adjust your pitch attitude in relation to the horizon, and then recheck the altimeter and vertical-speed indicator to make sure that altitude is being maintained.

During all turns, use the ailerons and rudder to correct minor variations, just as you do in straight-and-level flight.

Recovering from a turn, apply aileron and rudder pressures in the direction of the rollout or toward the raised wing. As the angle of bank decreases, smoothly release elevator pressure; it is no longer needed to maintain altitude.

Begin the turn recovery before reaching the desired new heading. The amount required to lead the heading depends upon the rate of turn and the rate at which you make the recovery. As the wings become level, gradually and smoothly release the control pressures so that they are neutralized as the airplane resumes straight-and-level flight. As the turn is completed, you should check your outside visual references as well as the attitude indicator and heading indicator.

Climbing and Descending Turns. When you are introduced to *climbing turns*, you'll need to consider the following factors:

- Without an increased power setting, the same pitch attitude and airspeed cannot be maintained in a bank as in a straight climb because of the decrease in both the effective lift and airspeed during a turn.
- The degree of bank should be neither too steep nor too shallow. Too steep of a bank intensifies the effect mentioned immediately above; too shallow, and the angle of bank will be difficult to maintain (because of the airplane's inherent stability).
- Strive for a constant airspeed, a constant rate of turn, and a constant angle of bank. It takes practice.
- As in all maneuvers, divert your attention from the airplane's nose. Divide it equally among all references.

There are two ways to establish a climbing turn. Either turn after the climb has been set up (following takeoff), or establish the pitch and bank attitudes simultaneously from straight-and-level flight.

The difficult thing about climbing turns is that you are coordinating all flight controls—pitch, roll, and yaw—simultaneously. Initially, you might have a little trouble applying the correct amount of rudder pressure because the adverse yaw tendency is magnified due to a climb's lower airspeed.

When attempting *descending turns,* in order to maintain the most efficient glide, more altitude must be sacrificed than in a straight glide because that is the only way airspeed can be maintained without power. However, skidding to the outside in a gliding turn, close to the ground, can be dangerous.

GROUND REFERENCE MANEUVERS

Ground reference maneuvers are sometimes looked upon with some displeasure by student pilots. I once heard a student characterize them as being "like finger exercises on a piano," implying that they were something his instructor had dreamed up in an evil moment, maneuvers never done in the "real world."

Well, yes and no. It is true that once you have earned your pilot certificate you may never again do S-turns across a road, or practice eights around pylons. But you will fly parts of these maneuvers. They will have given you a good "wind sense," and they certainly will have improved your coordination in handling two or more flight controls simultaneously. They may not be fun, but they are very useful.

As a prelude to a brief explanation of ground reference maneuvers (or "ground track" maneuvers, as they are sometimes called), I want to reiterate that the instant an airplane's wheels leave the ground the airplane—*any* airplane or other aircraft, large or small—is contained within the airmass that supports it. If that airmass is moving, it will carry the aircraft with it. While the aircraft will also move *through* the airmass at its normal speeds as controlled by the pilot, it will also be carried *with* the airmass if that airmass is moving.

This is sometimes confusing to student pilots, maybe because they are not primarily interested in maintaining a track through the airmass, but rather, maintaining a given track over the surface of the Earth below.

I once read a book manuscript about helicopter flying in which the author said that, hovering over a given spot on the ground, "a sidewind was blowing across the 'copter's rotor blades." The author did not understand that no wind can blow *across* a helicopter's rotors while the machine is in flight. The only way a helicopter can hover over a given spot when there is wind is by flying into the wind at an airspeed equal to the wind's velocity (although the fuselage might be oriented as much as 90° to the wind—a helicopter can fly sideways).

To an observer on the ground (and to the pilot), the chopper appears to be hanging motionless. It is not. It is moving into the wind, whatever the wind's direction. The only way that the wind can blow across its rotors, or strike it from any direction, is for the helicopter to land and rest on the ground. The same is true of fixed-wing aircraft. An aircraft in flight feels no wind because it is contained within the wind.

Some flight students grasp this basic fact immediately; others have trouble with it. Your practice of ground reference maneuvers will give you experience in countering wind effects while maintaining a desired track over the surface. It will be especially helpful in planning landing approaches.

Rectangular Course

The *rectangular course* (Fig. 4-1) is a practice maneuver in which the ground track of the aircraft is equidistant from all sides of a selected rectangular area on the ground. Such references are plentiful in the Plains, the Midwest, and other primarily agricultural areas of the country, because the surface is often laid out in neat, one-mile squares bounded by rural roads.

Like other ground reference maneuvers, one of the objectives is to develop division of attention between your flight path, ground references, and periodic instrument scan, while controlling the airplane and watching for other aircraft in the vicinity. Another objective is to develop recognition of drift toward or away from a line parallel to your intended ground track.

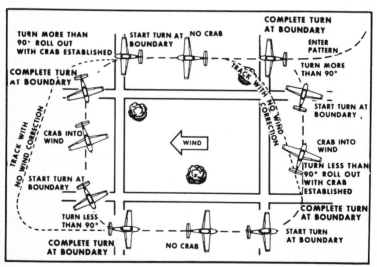

Fig. 4-1. The rectangular course practice maneuver helps to perfect your handling of the winds in an airport traffic pattern. In this example, the course is entered on the downwind leg.

Select a square or rectangular field, the sides of which are approximately one mile in length. You will fly this practice maneuver at a constant airspeed and altitude (600 to 1000 feet above the surface), and about one-fourth to one-half mile outside the boundaries of the reference. You will attempt to parallel these boundaries, at a uniform distance from each.

All turns should be started when the airplane is abeam the corners of the field boundaries, and the bank normally should not exceed 45°. These should be the determining factors in establishing the distance from the boundaries for performing the maneuver.

Let's assume that you will begin on the upwind leg (as opposed to the downwind entry depicted in Fig. 4-1). While flying the upwind leg, observe the next field boundary and plan your turn onto the crosswind leg. Because there is a headwind on this leg, it is retarding the airplane's ground speed, and during the turn onto the crosswind leg, the airplane will drift toward the field if you do not counter it. Your roll-in to the turn must, therefore, be slow and the bank relatively shallow. As the turn progresses, the headwind component decreases, allowing your ground speed to increase. Consequently, your bank angle and rate of turn must be gradually increased to assure that, upon completion of the turn, the crosswind ground track will continue the same distance from the edge of the field. Completion of the turn with the wings level should be accomplished at a point aligned with the upwind far corner of the reference field.

As the wings are rolled level, you must simultaneously establish the proper drift correction with the airplane "crabbed" into the wind. This requires that the turn be less than 90°. While on the crosswind leg this crab angle should be adjusted as necessary to maintain a uniform distance from the field boundary.

Since a crab angle is being held into the wind and away from the field while on the crosswind leg, the next turn will require a turn of more than 90°. Then the crosswind will become a tailwind, causing the ground speed to increase during this turn. The bank, initially, must be medium and progressively increased as the turn proceeds.

To complete the turn, the recovery must be timed so that the wings become level at a point aligned with that corner of the reference field. The distance from the field boundary should be the same as it was on the other side of the field.

On the downward leg the wind is a tailwind and results in an increased ground speed. Therefore, the turn onto the next leg must be entered with a fairly fast rate of roll into a relatively steep bank. As the turn progresses, the bank angle must be gradually reduced because the tailwind component is diminishing, resulting in a decreasing ground speed.

During and after this turn (equivalent to the base leg in a traffic pattern), the wind will tend to drift the airplane away from the field boundary. To compensate, the amount of turn must be more than 90°.

Recovery from this turn must be such that, as the wings become level, the airplane is crabbed slightly toward the field into the wind, to correct for the drift. Since you are holding drift correction on this leg, your next turn will be less than 90°. It will be a medium turn, with a gradual reduction in bank angle to shallow as the turn progresses.

It may be difficult to find a ground reference field with wind blowing exactly parallel to its boundaries, so you may have to crab slightly on all the legs. Two rules will help, whatever the wind: 1) When the wind is behind you, the turn must be faster and steeper; and 2) When the wind is head-on, the turn must be slower and shallower.

The turns are the keys and they require most of your effort and judgment. It is the downwind turn onto the base leg that is the most critical. This is the one that is most likely to get you into trouble—serious trouble at low altitude in an airport traffic pattern. Too many pilots have stalled out in this turn and, lacking the altitude to recover, have crashed.

Several factors might contribute to the insidious danger here:

1) You haven't much altitude in which to correct a mistake;
2) In moderate to strong winds, you have a lot of ground speed and are close enough to the ground to make that apparent. However, your airspeed—the only speed that matters to your wing—may be too low. (Therefore, you must reference your airspeed indicator and the ball in your turn indicator a couple of times as you enter this turn and, especially, as the turn progresses.)
3) Because you enter this turn with a faster rate of roll and it will be a relatively steep turn, you might be holding opposite rudder, along with substantial back pressure on the elevators. Crossed controls, combined with a low airspeed and high angle of attack, add up to a potentially dangerous situation.

4) If the bank is not steep enough to require opposite rudder, you can also get into trouble by using too much rudder in the direction of the turn, because a skid will drain away some lift.

5) You are turning more than 90°, which, in itself, may produce a tendency to rush or "over-tighten" the turn.

You must not allow yourself to over-concentrate on your ground track to the detriment of flying the airplane. Divide your attention between the outside ground references and the inside instrument references. After all, the wind affects *only* your ground speed and ground track. If you have to relax control pressures in order to maintain positive control of the airplane, do it.

S-Turns Across a Road

S-turns across a road, using a ground reference to make each "S" equal in size and uniformly proportioned, provide experience in compensating for wind through a series of opposing 180° turns. They also promote the habit of employing a scan which divides your attention between outside and inside references.

Select a straight stretch of road, with the wind blowing across the road at a 90° angle. The road will make a huge dollar sign ($) of your S-turns.

Assuming that the wind is from right-to-left in relation to your dollar sign, begin at the top of the S, 600 to 1000 feet above the surface, with the wind behind you.

When directly over the road, start the first turn immediately. With the airplane headed downwind, the ground speed is greatest and the rate of departure from the road is rapid, so roll into this steep bank fairly rapidly to minimize drift.

As you near the halfway point of this first 180° turn, the airplane's heading is changing from a downwind heading to a crosswind heading so the ground speed decreases. Begin to shallow the bank while noting that your crab angle at this point is greatest due to the crosswind component.

After turning 90°, your heading becomes more and more an upwind heading and your ground speed slows even more. Continue to gradually shallow the bank through the remaining 90° of the semicircle, so that the crab angle is completely removed and the wings become level as the 180° turn is completed at the moment you reach the road.

As you cross the road, start your turn in the opposite direction. Because you are flying into a headwind, your rate of roll will be slow and the bank shallow, at first. Then, turning from a crosswind to a downwind heading, the rate of turn must be progressively increased so that you will have turned 180° when you reach the road again. The altitude should remain constant throughout the S-turn, while the bank angle should be changing constantly in order to achieve a true semicircular ground track.

I want to make clear that when I say that downwind turns require a faster rate of roll and steeper bank than upwind turns, I am talking about maintaining a given track over the surface. When the object is merely to turn and fly another heading, and ground track is of no particular concern to you—which is most of the time— there is no reason to differentiate between downwind, crosswind, and upwind turns. They are all the same because the airplane feels no wind.

Some pilots never quite accept this. I have a friend who has flown at least 26 accident-free years. He is instrument-rated and does a lot of cross-country flying. Any time he has to make a heading change, and perceives that it involves a downwind turn, he adds a little power in that turn. It doesn't do any harm, but there is no valid reason why a downwind turn should be different from any other turn, unless you are low and trying to hold a definite track over the surface.

There are other ground reference maneuvers, including turns around a point, eights across a road, pylon eights, power-off descending 720s, etc. All emphasize practice in coordination of the controls and provide experience needed to hone your basic flying skills.

NOT-SO-NORMAL LANDINGS

At the end of our familiarization flight in Chapter 3, we made a "normal" landing—calm winds, smooth air, and a nice, long, hard-surfaced runway (without 500-kilovolt high-tension lines at each end).

In reality, such a landing is anything but "normal." You must be able to compensate for uncooperative winds, tooth-jarring turbulence, soggy farmyards, and anemic runways surrounded by factories and radio towers.

Landing in Crosswinds

Because Mother Nature has no regard for the directions in

which airport runways are built, you will make many crosswind landings.

There are two methods of accomplishing a crosswind approach and landing—the *crab* method and the *wing-low* method. Your instructor may teach you one or both, depending upon his or her preference.

The crab method is executed by establishing a heading slightly into the wind with wings level, while the airplane's ground track remains aligned with the centerline of the runway (Fig. 4-2). This

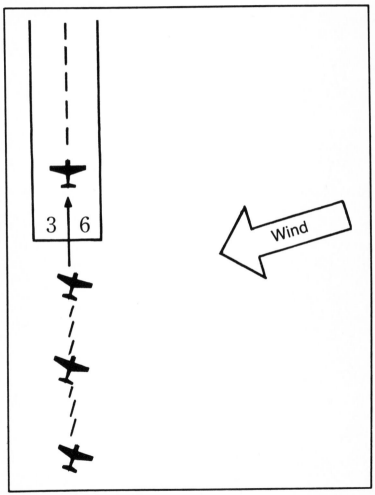

Fig. 4-2. The "crab" method of crosswind approach. Be sure to straighten out just before flare and touchdown.

crab angle is held until just prior to touchdown, when the airplane must be quickly aligned with the runway to avoid sideward contact of the wheels with the runway. The FAA suggests that if you are flying a long final approach, you should use the crab method until just before the flare and then smoothly change to the wing-low method for the remainder of the landing.

The wing-low method will compensate for a crosswind from any angle. It allows you to simultaneously keep the airplane's ground track and longitudinal axis aligned with the runway centerline throughout the final approach, touchdown, and rollout. It also eliminates the danger of touching down in a sideward attitude and imposing damaging side-loads on the landing gear.

In the wing-low method, you align the airplane with the runway's centerline, note the rate and direction of drift, and apply drift correction by lowering the upwind wing (Fig. 4-3). The amount the wing must be lowered depends upon the rate of drift.

When the wing is lowered, the airplane will, of course, tend to turn. It is necessary, therefore, to simultaneously apply sufficient opposite rudder pressure to keep the airplane aligned with the runway. In other words, the drift is controlled with aileron, the heading with rudder. The airplane will be side-slipping into the wind to maintain a flight path and ground track that is aligned with the runway.

If the required bank is so steep that full opposite rudder will not prevent a turn, the wind is too strong to safely land the airplane on the runway, and you must find a runway that is better aligned with the wind—if not at that airport, then at an alternate airport.

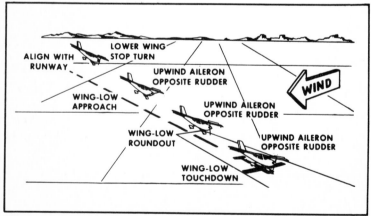

Fig. 4-3. Crosswind approach and landing: the wing-low method.

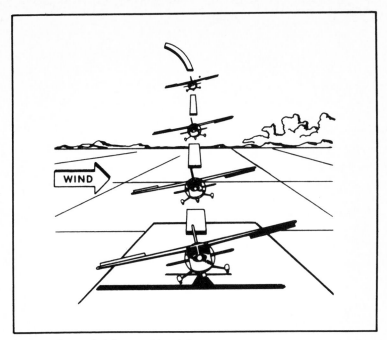

Fig. 4-4. Crosswind flare and touchdown.

The *flare* (or *roundout*, as it is sometimes called) can be made as usual, but you must continue the crosswind correction (Fig. 4-4). Since your airspeed decreases throughout the flare, your flight controls become less effective and it will be necessary to increase control pressures on the rudder and aileron to maintain the proper amount of drift correction.

Do not level the wings; keep the upwind wing down throughout the flare and touchdown. You'll touch down on one wheel, but do not lift your upwind wing to put the other main wheel on the ground. As forward momentum decreases after initial contact, the weight of the airplane will cause the downwind main wheel to gradually settle onto the runway.

The crab method is easier and more comfortable to maintain, except for the final instant before touchdown when it requires a high degree of judgment and good timing to remove the crab angle and contact the surface with the airplane pointed straight down the runway. The wing-low method allows you to keep the airplane's nose pointed straight down the runway throughout your final approach, and you touch down on one wheel. All things considered, it is probably the easier of the two.

Regardless of which method you use, after the main gear are down, hold the nosewheel off as usual. In those airplanes having nosewheel steering interconnected with the rudder, the nosewheel may not be aligned with the runway because opposite rudder is being held in the crosswind correction. To prevent a swerve in the direction the nosewheel is pointed, the corrective rudder pressure must be promptly relaxed just as the nosewheel is allowed to come down. In crosswind conditions, you might want to put the nosewheel down a little earlier than normal—but at least wait until both mains are rolling.

Some airplanes have a centering cam built into the nose gear strut to keep the nosewheel straight until the strut is compressed upon touchdown. Nevertheless, you will still relax rudder pressure as the nosewheel touches because it will require less corrective action to track down the runway centerline guiding with the nosewheel than it did with only the rudder during the last seconds just prior to touchdown.

During rollout, you will continue to keep the control wheel turned into the wind, and as you decelerate and your ailerons become less effective you will have to increase aileron pressure. By the time the airplane comes to a stop, you should have the control wheel turned fully toward the wind.

As you slow down during rollout, the crosswind becomes stronger in proportion to your forward velocity. Because an airplane has more vertical surface (exposed to the crosswind) behind the main wheels than ahead of them, the plane has an increasing tendency to pivot into the wind, or *weathervane*. Therefore, you need to continue to use rudder as necessary to maintain your desired track down the runway.

The maximum safe crosswind component is given in the airplane's operating manual, and it is the pilot's business to know it for each airplane he flies.

Landing in Turbulent Air

In significantly turbulent air, power-on approaches are best, usually at the normal approach speed plus one-half the wind gust factor, or whatever speed the airplane's operations manual lists for such conditions. (The throttle will be retarded to idle only after the mains are rolling.) This allows more positive control of the airplane when strong horizontal or vertical gusts are encountered.

Since you are carrying a little extra airspeed, you can make minor altitude adjustments with pitch, and control airspeed with power. But, as always, such trade-offs are limited, and a coordinated *combination* of pitch and power adjustments are usually called for.

Partial flaps may be helpful. With less than full flaps the nose will be higher, landing attitude will require less of a pitch change, and the touchdown will be at a higher airspeed to ensure more positive control.

In severe turbulence, landings from power approaches should be accomplished with the airplane in an almost level attitude at touchdown. Hold the nose up just enough to keep the nosewheel off until the mains are on, and then relax back pressure on the wheel to allow the nosewheel to come down. Don't allow the nosewheel to touch first. Combined with your extra speed, that can cause a condition euphemistically known as *wheelbarrowing,* which can prove to be very interesting, requiring some artful corrective measures (and a little luck) to avoid bending the airplane.

If you fly a tailwheel airplane the approach is the same. Touch down on the main wheels in a level attitude under these conditions. Retard the throttle as soon as both mains are on the ground, and hold enough forward pressure on the control wheel (or stick) to keep them on the ground. The trick here is never to force the airplane onto the ground with a lot of nose-down control pressure, but to "grease" the wheels on carefully. Otherwise, the airplane will have a tendency to bounce back into the air. Attempts to control the bounce usually aggravate the situation because the airplane is "ahead of you" and, in most cases, you'll go *porpoising* down the runway with each bounce worse than the last. The best action is to open the throttle and go around for another try.

Porpoising, by the way, is not a condition limited to tailwheel airplanes. You can get the same unhappy results in a tricycle-gear airplane if you force the mains on the ground at a high sink rate and then try to catch up with the bounces.

Landing on Soft Fields

When landing on fields that are rough or have soft surfaces, such as snow, sand, mud, or tall grass, you will want the wings to support the weight of the airplane as long as possible in order to minimize stresses on the landing gear. Approach to a *soft-field landing* is the same as a normal approach, except that after flare, you will hold the airplane a foot or two off the ground as long as possible with increasing back pressure on the control wheel to bleed off airspeed and allow the wheels to touch down very softly, and with the nose high. Hold the nosewheel off as long as you can. Do not use brakes; you probably won't need them. In fact, on very soft ground, you may need to apply power to keep the airplane moving. For obvious reasons, taildraggers have a definite advantage over other airplanes when operating off of soft fields.

Landing on Short Fields

On occasion, you will need to land on runways that aren't much longer than the distance needed to stop your airplane. *Short-field landings* are achieved by landing at a minimum safe speed that allows sufficient margin above stall and provides good control, along with the capability for a go-around. Generally, the landing speed is a fixed percentage of the stall speed (or minimum control speed) with the airplane in landing configuration.

The techniques used to achieve minimum landing distance and those of an ordinary landing roll (with considerable excess runway available) are different. Minimum landing distance requires the extensive use of brakes. On the other hand, on an ordinary landing roll you can use aerodynamic drag to minimize wear and tear on the tires and brakes.

In our training airplane, aerodynamic braking during landing is achieved by using flaps and by holding the nose high during the first part of the rollout. Because aerodynamic braking is ineffective below 60 to 70 percent of the touchdown speed, you should retract flaps as soon as you estimate that 30 to 40 percent of your speed has dissipated; this gets rid of whatever extra lift they are generating and transfers that load to the main wheels. On unimproved airstrips, it also reduces the chance of damage to the flaps from pebbles or other debris kicked up by the propeller or wheels, especially in low-wing airplanes. As the flaps are retracted, you may lower the nose.

The *usual* advice to student pilots is to "hold the nosewheel off as long as practicable." And there are good reasons for holding the nosewheel off after touchdown: to save the nosewheel assembly, and especially its mounting, from high loadings; to reduce tire wear; and to take advantage of the aerodynamic braking provided by the nose-high configuration.

But there are also reasons for wanting the nosewheel down and rolling. It permits positive steering after the rudder loses effectiveness. It reduces the lift remaining in the wings. And it needs to be down before wheel brakes are applied.

If you watch a number of lightplanes on landing rollout you'll note that some pilots seem to put the nosewheel on the runway very soon after their mains are rolling, and others seem to hold it off as long as they can.

If that seems confusing, just remember that your main concern is not the nosewheel *per se*, but simply to put the airplane on the ground under *positive control* and at a safe minimum airspeed. Wind, as well as runway length and condition, can alter technique.

You might be surprised to learn how many accidents occur during landing rollout. These accidents don't produce a lot of injuries to people, but they do damage a lot of flying machines and underscore the wisdom contained in the old saying, "You're flying it until it's in the hangar."

EMERGENCY LANDINGS

Chances are that you will never be faced with the need to make an emergency landing. Modern airplanes and their engines, properly maintained, are extremely reliable, and good planning in their operation practically eliminates the possibility of being forced down by fuel exhaustion or unexpected weather, while the electronic revolution has left today's pilot with little excuse for getting lost.

Nevertheless, you should be prepared to cope with the need to make an immediate off-airport landing. It can happen.

The National Transportation Safety Board has found several factors that might interfere with a pilot's ability to act promptly and properly when faced with such an emergency:

- Reluctance to accept the emergency situation: A pilot who allows his mind to become paralyzed at the thought that the airplane will be on the ground in a short time, regardless of what is done, is severely handicapped in the handling of the emergency. An unconscious desire to delay this dreaded moment may lead to such errors as failure to lower the nose to maintain flying speed, delay in selection of the most suitable landing area within reach, and indecision in general.

- Desire to save the airplane: A pilot who has been conditioned to expect to find a relatively safe landing area whenever his instructor closed the throttle for a simulated forced landing may ignore all basic rules of airmanship to avoid landing in terrain where aircraft damage is unavoidable. The desire to save the airplane, regardless of the risks involved, may be influenced by the pilot's financial stake in the machine, and the certainty that an undamaged airplane implies no bodily harm as well. There are times when a pilot should be more interested in sacrificing the aircraft so that all occupants can safely walk away from it.

- Undue concern about getting hurt: Fear is a vital part of man's self-preservation instinct. But when fear leads to panic he invites that which he wants most to avoid.

Flying cross-country, develop the habit of noting suitable forced-landing fields. Punctuate your normal scan (begin behind one wing, move leisurely across the instrument panel, hesitate there to look ahead and above, and continue to behind the opposite wing) with confirmation of surface checkpoints when appropriate, and note possible forced-landing fields while determining surface wind direction from smoke stacks, blowing dust, etc.

The perfect forced-landing field is an established airport, or a hard-packed, long, smooth field with no high obstacles on the approach end. However, these ideal conditions may not be readily available, so the best available field must be selected. Cultivated fields are usually satisfactory, and plowed fields are acceptable if the landing is made parallel to the furrows.

Keep in mind that a downwind landing will add more to your landing rollout than a comparable headwind subtracts from it, but don't insist upon landing into the wind if that requires maneuvering that you might not have the altitude to accomplish. Your main objective is an acceptable field that you can safely reach under positive control. Obstacles to the approach might be more important than wind direction (Fig. 4-5).

The more altitude you have when an emergency becomes evident, the more flexibility you will have in selecting a place to land. If you can make your selection with plenty of excess altitude, circle directly above the spot while looking for obstacles such as utility poles (you can't see utility *wires* from the air; they blend into the darker background of the surface), livestock, ditches, etc.

When the engine stops you should immediately go through your failed-engine drill, the first item of which is to establish a maximum-distance glide. (The airplane's operating manual lists the maximum-glide airspeed; it's a figure you should check before flying any airplane.)

You should maintain a constant gliding speed because it is important in judging your gliding distance and determining your touchdown spot. You will control the glide speed with pitch.

Next, check the fuel selector to make sure that it is turned to

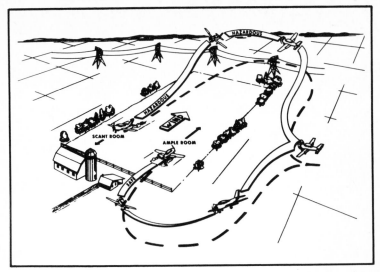

Fig. 4-5. In an emergency, a downwind landing can sometimes be the safest.

a tank containing fuel. The other things you will do might differ slightly in different airplanes, but as a general rule, they will follow the procedure illustrated in Fig. 4-6.

If an engine failure occurs immediately after takeoff and before a safe maneuvering altitude is attained, it is usually not advisable

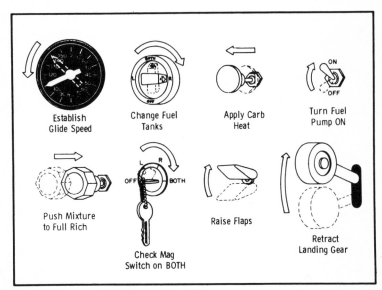

Establish Glide Speed

Change Fuel Tanks

Apply Carb Heat

Turn Fuel Pump ON

Push Mixture to Full Rich

Check Mag Switch on BOTH

Raise Flaps

Retract Landing Gear

Fig. 4-6. Typical engine failure checklist.

to try to turn back to the field from which the takeoff was made. In most cases it is safer to immediately get the nose down, establish the proper glide attitude, and select a field directly ahead, or slightly to either side, of your takeoff path.

It isn't easy to continue straight ahead under such conditions. However, if you attempt to make a 180° turn to get back to the runway you just left, that downwind turn will increase your ground speed and rush you in planning. Meanwhile, the airplane will be losing considerable altitude, possibly striking the ground during the turn. So the straight-ahead option is usually more attractive, even if it means certain damage to the airplane. There is an old saying in flying that nothing is more useless than the runway behind you and the altitude above.

In the above discussion, the two main points that emerge are: first, always maintain positive control of the airplane, and second, be prepared—through training, practice, and forethought—to make the correct decision, whatever the situation. Throughout your flying career, in every possible situation, your primary concern is to *fly the airplane*.

Back during World War II, a story circulated around one of the training fields about a solo student who wrecked an airplane in an off-airport landing. When called before his commanding officer to explain, he said, "Well, sir, I picked a nice-looking field and I made a good approach. Then, as I was about to touch down, I saw that ditch. So, I shut my eyes and said, 'God, you take over now!' Geez! I coulda done better myself!"

That story probably isn't true, but it does point up a certain truth: That cadet surely could have done better by maintaining control. More than one pilot has saved himself and his passengers from injury by guiding his crippled machine between two trees when no better forced-landing spot was available. In such cases, the wings depart the aircraft rather suddenly, but the cabin usually remains intact.

Flight Plans. A *flight plan* is a form you'll fill out prior to takeoff and file with the nearest Flight Service Station (FSS). It lists your route, destination, aircraft identification, and other pertinent data about your trip (Fig. 4-7). If there's no FSS at your departure point you can file a flight plan by telephone or radio.

A flight plan is not required for VFR flights, but for extended cross-country trips, especially over rough or sparsely populated terrain, you should always file a flight plan. Then, if you are ever forced down, the Civil Air Patrol's search-and-rescue people will

U.S. DEPARTMENT OF TRANSPORTATION FEDERAL AVIATION ADMINISTRATION **FLIGHT PLAN**	(FAA USE ONLY) ☐ PILOT BRIEFING ☐ STOPOVER	☐ VNR	TIME STARTED	SPECIALIST INITIALS

1. TYPE ☐ VFR ☐ IFR ☐ DVFR	2 AIRCRAFT IDENTIFICATION	3 AIRCRAFT TYPE/ SPECIAL EQUIPMENT	4 TRUE AIRSPEED KTS	5 DEPARTURE POINT	6 DEPARTURE TIME PROPOSED (Z) · ACTUAL (Z)	7 CRUISING ALTITUDE

8 ROUTE OF FLIGHT

9 DESTINATION (Name of airport and city)	10 EST. TIME ENROUTE HOURS · MINUTES	11 REMARKS

12 FUEL ON BOARD HOURS · MINUTES	13 ALTERNATE AIRPORT(S)	14 PILOT'S NAME, ADDRESS & TELEPHONE NUMBER & AIRCRAFT HOME BASE 17 DESTINATION CONTACT/TELEPHONE (OPTIONAL)	15 NUMBER ABOARD

16 COLOR OF AIRCRAFT	CIVIL AIRCRAFT PILOTS. FAR Part 91 requires you file an IFR flight plan to operate under instrument flight rules in controlled airspace. Failure to file could result in a civil penalty not to exceed $1,000 for each violation (Section 901 of the Federal Aviation Act of 1958, as amended). Filing of a VFR flight plan is recommended as a good operating practice. See also Part 99 for requirements concerning DVFR flight plans.

FAA Form 7233-1 (8-82)   CLOSE VFR FLIGHT PLAN WITH_____ FSS ON ARRIVAL

Fig. 4-7. Flight plan. Be sure to close your flight plan promptly upon reaching your destination—or an alternate. If you don't, a search will begin automatically.

be out looking for you within a few hours. Make sure that you close your flight plan upon reaching your destination or an alternate. Otherwise, a search begins automatically, 30 minutes after your scheduled arrival time.

Emergency Locator Transmitters. Federal Aviation Regulations require that airplanes flying cross-country be equipped with *emergency locator transmitters* (ELTs). The ELT, usually installed somewhere in the airplane's tail, is battery-operated and crash-activated. When armed and subjected to crash forces, it emits a distinctive downward-swept audio tone on 121.5 MHz and 243.0 MHz. ELTs are designed to continuously transmit for at least 48 hours over a wide temperature range.

Airborne tests of ELTs are unlawful for obvious reasons, and caution should be exercised to prevent inadvertent activation while they are being handled on the ground. The FAA encourages pilots to monitor ELT frequencies while in flight. In practice, American and Soviet earth satellites, have proven unexpectedly useful in receiving ELT signals.

EMERGENCY INSTRUMENT PROCEDURES

It is possible that the time may come when you'll find yourself—purely by accident, of course—smack in the middle of instrument weather conditions. Naturally, you don't *intend* to be caught "on the gauges"—at least not until you've got some experience behind you and have trained for an instrument rating—but weather forecasting is not an exact science.

The other factor is human nature. Let's take a typical example: A pilot has planned with his wife and another couple to fly interstate over the weekend for a big football game. The tickets were expensive and hard to come by. The gals have been excited about the trip for days. Then, at 7 A.M. Saturday morning when our pilot calls the FSS, he learns of a low pressure area lying across the flight path about 300 miles out. It's CAVU (ceiling and visibility unlimited) at both ends, but in between is an area fifty miles wide of low ceilings and freezing rain. The cloud base, however, is forecast to lift above VFR minimums later in the day.

So our little party, with spirits undimmed, drives to the airport, and the passengers stow thermoses and stadium blankets in the airplane in happy anticipation, while our pilot runs over to the FSS for another weather check. Nothing has changed, but the weather people are still optimistic. Our party goes to the terminal for coffee and to kill a little time. There's still time to catch an airline flight, but somehow, that opportunity slips by. At 9 A.M. that distant patch of bad weather appears to be lifting a little, the weatherman says, but at the moment, it's still strictly IFR.

Gosh, how our pilot friend hates to disappoint his wife and their best friends! Besides, it's clear that their estimation of his flying ability is going to go down considerably if he refuses to go.

Finally, at 10 A.M., with the weatherman still very doubtful (". . . perhaps later this afternoon . . ."), our pilot makes his decision. The stuff is lifting a little, and anyway, if they can't get underneath they can surely get through a little patch of rain and clouds only twenty minutes or so wide. True, he's not instrument rated, but he's been flying for two years and has almost 300 hours in his logbook. Also, the weather *has* been improving during the past several hours, and is bound to improve further by the time they reach it. He tells everyone to get aboard. The game starts at 2 P.M.

But game time really doesn't make any difference. They never get there. Civil Air Patrol search planes find the wreckage before dark. The newspapers carry the story the next day.

Sure, it's depressing. I advise that you remember it. A similar situation is repeated a dozen times or more every year. I hope you'll never be a party to it (Fig. 4-8).

Apparently acting upon the theory that people are people and will, on occasion, make poor decisions in the face of their better

Fig. 4-8. Never allow "get-there-itis" to overrule your better judgment. Almost 40 percent of all lightplane accidents are weather-related.

judgment, the FAA has attempted to cut the accident rate of noninstrument pilots "pushing the weather" by requiring that, as part of the private pilot's flight test, you demonstrate an ability to maintain control of your airplane by reference to instruments alone.

This is not to say that you must have an instrument rating, or even that an instrument rating is practical or desirable for everyone. But a few hours' dual instruction in instrument flying is required by the FARs before you can take your private pilot's flight test. It will not be sufficient to qualify you for an instrument rating; it is intended only to provide you with the minimum skill needed to get you out of trouble if you stumble into instrument flight conditions.

In most cases, when you are accidentally caught on instruments, clear weather will lie behind you—from where you have just come. Therefore, by simply turning around and flying a reciprocal course you will return to VFR conditions. It's simple, but not quite as simple as it sounds.

Here's why: Once you've lost visual contact with the ground, your senses of balance and direction—including your up-and-down sense—are gone. Non-fliers find this hard to believe (and so have some fliers who are no longer with us), but it is true. Instrument instructors are familiar with the novice who, when first exposed to instrument flight, leans far to one side, unconsciously straining against a banking condition that does not exist. The student's sense of equilibrium, when he is denied a look at the ground, falsely tells him he is banking. The instruments know better, though it takes a while for most of us to place our trust where it is deserved—even with life at stake.

This brings up the first and, perhaps, most important rule: *Always believe your instruments.* If your turn needle says that you are turning, then no matter what the seat-of-your-pants says, *believe the turn needle.*

This is the central fact to be learned in controlling your plane without visual reference to the ground. Your nervous system will lie to you. Know this, and believe only the impersonal, nerveless instruments. It's true that your nervous system has the feel of the controls and "knows" how to fly the plane—but only as long as your eyes are feeding it the necessary reference points. You have no feel for the earth when your feet are not firmly planted upon it. You are supported in an ocean of air by that wing out there—and the only thing that matters to it is its angle of attack.

Most non-instrument pilots get into serious trouble within a minute or so after flying into instrument weather; a wing drops slightly. This causes the airplane to start a gentle turn. Next, the nose drops a little to make up for the loss of lift due to the unsuspected bank. Finally, the pilot, noticing his increasing airspeed, pulls back on the wheel. But as you know, back pressure on the wheel pulls the nose up, increasing the angle of attack. Pulling the nose up in a downward spiral only tightens the spiral because the wings are not level. At this point, the pilot is only seconds away from becoming a statistic.

Yep, I'm back to the depressing prose again. But again, remember it—it's *your* neck I'm talking about, and I want to impress upon you the importance of your turn needle (or turn coordinator) any time you are without visual ground contact. Keep that turn needle centered; then a wing can't get down unnoticed to start this fatal pattern. (A turn coordinator uses an airplane figure in place of a needle. Leveling the wings of the airplane figure is the same as centering the needle.)

Under these conditions, you can ignore the slip-and-skid indicator, because you don't care how much you skid in holding your wings level. What you're interested in is positive control until you can get VFR again.

So the second rule is: *Hold the wings level by reference to the turn needle (or turn coordinator).*

All right, that takes care of directional attitude control, holding the wings level. But you also want to hold the nose level. The instrument you use for this is the airspeed indicator, but you interpret it differently from the turn indicator. Whereas you keep the turn needle exactly centered (or average-center in rough air), you need to watch the airspeed's *tendency* to keep the nose level. If the airspeed needle is moving up the scale, indicating higher readings, you are in a nose-down attitude, diving. The faster it winds up, the steeper your dive. Conversely, if the airspeed needle is moving backward, showing a decreasing airspeed, then you are in a nose-high attitude. The speed with which the needle drops back is an indication of how steeply your nose is pointed upward (Fig. 4-9).

But as long as the airspeed needle remains at a constant speed, your nose is level (assuming flaps up and cruise power setting). Check the altimeter to be sure.

In all cases, use light, relaxed (okay, so who's relaxed at a time like this?) control pressures on the wheel and rudder pedals. Overcontrolling can become a vicious circle.

Now that you know how to keep the airplane straight-and-level and under control, the next thing is to turn around 180° and go back (or to an alternate that is reporting VFR conditions).

First, what is your reciprocal heading? (If you did a good job of flight planning before takeoff, you won't be forced to do mental arithmetic under pressure now. You'll not only have the figure ready, but a heading to an alternate as well.) It's 320°? Okay. Apply a little rudder pressure, just enough to move the turn needle a distance equal to its width (it has a blunt end, and this is easy to judge accurately). A "one-needle-width" turn is equal to three degrees of turn per second. This means that your 180-degree turn to reciprocal will take exactly one minute. To achieve the same turn using a turn coordinator, apply enough rudder pressure to cause the little airplane figure to bank so that its wingtip aligns with the standard-rate-of-turn index at the edge of the instrument (Fig. 4-10).

The third rule, therefore, is: *A needle-width turn continued for one minute equals a 180-degree change in direction.*

At the end of of one minute, center the turn needle again and, as soon as the magnetic compass settles down, check to see if you've hit your desired 320-degree reciprocal. If not, use a little rudder to make the necessary slight correction. Some instructors prefer to teach a "one-half-needle-width" turn. This results in a 180-degree change of direction in two minutes, because the rate of turn is 1½

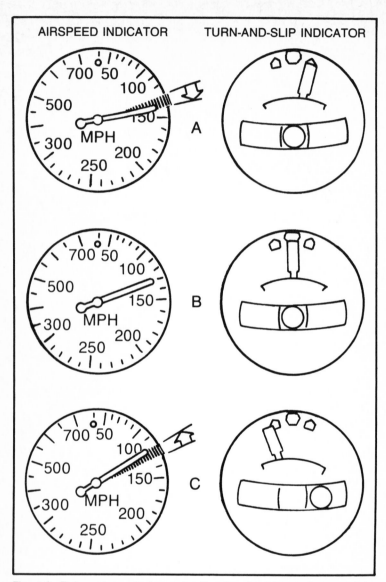

AIRSPEED INDICATOR   TURN-AND-SLIP INDICATOR

Fig. 4-9. Flying on two instruments: Reading from top to bottom, three representative readings in an airplane with a normal cruise of 145 MPH (IAS). Immediately upon finding ourselves in an instrument situation, we reduced RPM about 10 percent to give us an IAS of 130 MPH. If we later find the two instruments looking like A, we know we are in a spiral. Can you see why? At B we have properly recovered; first, we centered the turn needle, then we stabilized the airspeed with pitch. At C we have a different problem. The nose is high, and we are turning to the left. We are also skidding, but forgot the ball. All we are interested in is centering the needle and stabilizing the airspeed.

Fig. 4-10. Read the turn coordinator as you would the needle in the old turn-and-slip indicator. The turn coordinator does not indicate pitch.

degrees per second. Its advantage is that it is a gentler turn under these trying conditions; its disadvantage is that it prolongs the agony.

Either way, an important point to remember in this method of attitude control is to follow the sequence: First, center the turn needle; second, steady the airspeed needle. Repeat these two things over and over again until you are VFR.

The chief value of this method lies in its simplicity. Forget trim. Changes of trim under these conditions can give the non-instrument pilot more trouble than benefit. In fact, anything that takes your full attention away from the turn needle and airspeed must be regarded as extraneous activity until you are out of the soup. Nor should it be necessary to adjust the throttle more than once. Immediately upon finding yourself on instruments, set the throttle about 10 percent below normal cruise. That will slow you down a little and ease wing loadings if turbulence is present. Also, it will slow down the airspeed needle's gains or losses, making these tendencies easier to correct without overcontrolling.

Summing up the important points:

1) Reduce throttle setting to about 10 percent below normal cruise.
2) Center the turn needle.

3) Steady the airspeed needle.
4) Endlessly repeat points 2 and 3.
5) A one-needle-width turn, continued for one minute, equals a 180-degree change in direction.

It is possible, due to unusual turbulence or even panic, to lose control temporarily after stumbling into instrument weather. If this should happen, the attitude control method explained above is still the quickest and safest way for a non-instrument pilot to regain command of the airplane. First—*everlastingly first*—center the turn needle. But if the plane has gotten away from you and is diving at high speed, you should close the throttle before easing the wheel back. As the airspeed drops back to near normal, you will feed in power again. Then repeat the critical one-two sequence: Center the turn needle; steady the airspeed needle.

A great advantage of this system of attitude control is that it works well even in planes possessing a bare minimum of instrumentation.

Chapter 5

Weather

THE FAA MAINTAINS a nationwide network of Flight Service Stations (FSS) to serve the weather data needs of general-aviation pilots. By 1995, local FSSs will be replaced by regional automated stations (AFSSs); several of these are already in place. They are accessible by a single nationwide toll-free telephone number. For the next few years, however, many pilots can continue to rely on in-person weather briefings provided by the specialists at the FSSs. Normally, the FSS should be your last stop (or phone call) prior to takeoff for a cross-country flight (well, next-to-last stop).

Your home television can also provide you with a generalized weather picture, if not by way of your local stations, then via the Weather Channel (cable) or "A.M. Weather" on PBS. But these sources are not substitutes for an official weather briefing.

The Transcribed Weather Broadcast (TWEB), telephone access to the TWEB (TEL-TWEB), and Pilots' Automatic Telephone Weather Answering Service (PATWAS), give continuously updated recorded weather information for short or local flights. If you have a Touch-Tone telephone and live in one of 24 large cities, you can obtain some limited computerized weather data through the Interim Voice Response System (IVRS). Phone numbers for these services are listed in the FAA's *Airport/Facility Directory*, and under the FAA and National Weather Service (NWS) telephone numbers (U.S. Government listings) in your local telephone directory. Your local FBO will have the numbers if there is no FSS on the field.

In-flight weather information is available by radio from any FSS.

PREFLIGHT WEATHER BRIEFINGS

Three kinds of preflight weather briefings are available at the FSS: the Standard, Abbreviated, and Outlook briefings. Tell the specialist which type you want, along with the background information about your proposed flight that he needs to give you a personal briefing.

- **Standard Briefing.** You should request a Standard Briefing any time you are planning a flight and have not received a previous briefing, or have not received preliminary information through TWEB or PATWAS. The specialist will automatically provide the following information when it is applicable to your proposed flight:
    1. Adverse Conditions—Significant meteorological and aeronautical information that might influence you to alter your proposed flight plan, e.g., hazardous weather, runway closures, navaid outages, etc.
    2. VFR Flight Not Recommended—When VFR flight is proposed, and sky conditions or visibilities are present or forecast, surface or aloft, that in the specialist's judgment would make flight under VFR doubtful, the specialist will describe the conditions, affected locations, and use the phrase, "VFR flight is not recommended." This is advisory in nature. The final decision as to whether the flight can be conducted safely rests solely with the pilot (FAR 91.3a).
    3. Synopsis—A brief statement describing the type, location, and movement of weather systems and/or air masses which might affect the proposed flight.
    4. Current Conditions.
    5. En Route Forecast.
    6. Destination Forecast.
    7. Winds Aloft.
    8. NOTAMs (Notices to Airmen).
    9. ATC Delays.
    10. Other Information (upon request)—(a.) Information on military training routes and Military Operations Area

(MOA) activity within 100 nautical miles (NM) of the facility conducting the briefing. (b.) Approximate density altitude data. (c.) Information regarding such items as air traffic services and rules, customs/immigration procedures, ADIZ rules (Air Defense Identification Zones along U.S. coasts), search and rescue, etc.

- **Abbreviated Briefing.** Request an Abbreviated Briefing when you need information to supplement previously obtained data, or when you need only one or two specific items. Tell the briefer what information you have and how old it is.
- **Outlook Briefing.** Request an Outlook Briefing when your proposed time of departure is six or more hours from the time of the briefing. This type of briefing is for planning purposes only. A Standard or Abbreviated Briefing should follow prior to takeoff.
- **In-Flight Briefing.** You are encouraged to obtain your briefing by telephone or in person before departure, but in those cases where you need to obtain an initial briefing (or an update to a previous briefing) in flight, you should contact the nearest FSS by radio.

Always save your questions until the briefing has been completed.

EN ROUTE FLIGHT ADVISORY SERVICE

Known as "Flight Watch," this service is specifically designed to provide en-route aircraft with timely and meaningful advisories pertinent to the type of flight intended, route of flight, and altitude. It is normally available from 6 A.M. to 10 P.M..

Flight Watch is not intended to be used for filing or closing flight plans, position reporting, or to obtain a complete weather briefing. But it does serve as a clearinghouse for pilot-reported weather information. You are encouraged to report good, bad, expected, and unexpected flight conditions.

To contact a Flight Watch facility, use 122.0 MHz and the name of the VOR nearest to you. For example, "Washington Flight Watch, Cessna One Three Two Four Kilo, Westminster VOR, over."

IN-FLIGHT WEATHER ADVISORIES

The National Weather Service issues in-flight weather

advisories designated as Convective SIGMETs, SIGMETs, and AIRMETs.

Convective SIGMETs are issued for tornadoes, lines of thunderstorms, thunderstorms embedded in other cloud cover, and areas with 40 percent or more of thunderstorm activity.

SIGMETs are issued for severe and extreme turbulence, severe icing, and widespread dust storms.

AIRMETs are issued for moderate icing, moderate turbulence, sustained winds of 30 knots or more at the surface, widespread areas with ceilings less than 1,000 feet and/or visibility less than three miles, as well as extensive mountain obscurement.

SIGMETs and AIRMETs have a phonetic letter designator followed by a number (e.g., SIGMET Bravo 1). Succeeding advisories retain the same alphabetic designator as long as that particular weather condition exists, but the number changes in order to establish how recent each is. Alpha through November are used only for SIGMETs, while designators Oscar through Zulu are used for AIRMETs. SIGMETs and AIRMETs are announced by radio from FSSs and are also sent out over the weather teletype system.

As you can see, the FAA and National Weather Service expend considerable effort trying to keep you out of trouble with the weather. You can also help yourself by learning some weather basics.

AIR PRESSURE

At sea level, air weighs about 1¼ ounces per cubic foot and presses down with a pressure of about 14.7 pounds per square inch. This will cause mercury in a vacuum tube to rise 29.92 inches under standard conditions. So we consider a barometric reading of 29.92″ Hg (inches of mercury) as the reference or starting point for any fluctuation in pressure.

You need to be concerned with this not only because several of your most important flight instruments are pressure instruments, but because variations in air pressure are linked with variations in weather.

If temperatures remained constant there wouldn't be pressure variations, but of course they don't. The Sun heats the Earth's surface unequally. Different kinds of terrain absorb or reflect heat rays differently.

For example, a portion of the Earth's surface, such as a wheat field, may absorb relatively more heat from the Sun than the land surrounding it. The air immediately above the wheat field becomes warmer than the surrounding air, expands, and as it becomes lighter, starts to rise. This rising column of air is called a *thermal* or *convection current*. Often, it will rise until its moisture condenses and makes a cumulus cloud. Meanwhile, the rising, expanding air has created a tiny low pressure area at its base, and the relatively cooler, higher-pressure air surrounding it wants to rush in and equalize things. Thus, a wind is born.

A similar process, on a vastly bigger scale, creates the huge low pressure areas that move across the earth's face "making weather."

High pressure areas exist for just the opposite reasons. Air gets denser and heavier when it is cooled. Cool air is stable* and clear. This is why, as a flier, you will normally associate highs with good flying conditions, and suspect lows of harboring or generating bad weather.

When we speak of "warm" and "cool" air in this context, the meaning of the adjectives is relative. If the temperature at a given place is 90° F, and that area is surrounded with 85° F air, then 85° F is "cool."

The winds around a low are counterclockwise; around a high, the rotation is clockwise. This is because the higher pressure air surrounding a low, which flows inward to equalize the pressure, is deflected to one side by the Earth's west-to-east rotation. The air moving outward from a high is also given a twist by the Earth's spin, causing these winds to blow opposite to those around a low. These processes are reversed south of the equator.

FRONTS AND AIR MASSES

There are really only two basic kinds of air masses: *tropical* and *polar*. In order to know what to expect when one starts moving, however, the weather people further classify them according to the route they travel and their relative temperatures (i.e., a "polar continental cold air mass"). Their route is significant because air flowing over continents will not pick up moisture like air traveling over oceans will. Therefore, when an air mass begins to move, the weatherman tags it first according to its origin and second according

---

*Stable air, to the weatherman, is air in which cumulus will not build up into thunderheads. Student pilots sometimes assume that bumpy air is "unstable," although just the opposite may be the case. For example, the cool air behind a front may be bumpy—it usually is—but it is stable.

to its route. Third, he labels it "warm" or "cold," in relation to the temperature of the air it is overtaking. From these characteristics its behavior may be forecast.

When an air mass starts moving, it often produces a *front*, an almost definite line along its foremost part which separates it from the air of different temperature that it is overtaking (there is surprisingly little mixing of the air when two masses come together).

A *cold front* is the transitional area between a mass of advancing cool air and the warmer air in its path (Fig. 5-1).

A cold front has a wedge-shaped leading edge (when viewed in cross-section) because, being relatively heavy, it pushes under the warmer air in its path. The warmer air, being forced upward, tends to condense and form clouds—high cumulus and thunderheads—and rain or snow can be expected (depending upon the amount of moisture present). Behind the front is stable and heavy air with good visibility.

A *warm front* is the transitional area between an advancing mass of warm air and a retreating mass of cooler air (Fig. 5-2). The leading edge of a warm front rides up over the cooler air in its path. Warm fronts, too, bring a change in weather—usually precipitation in some form and a wind shift. But unlike cold fronts, overcast skies and unstable air remain.

On weather maps, only the ground-level leading edge of a front is shown. In the case of a warm front, the very foremost edge of

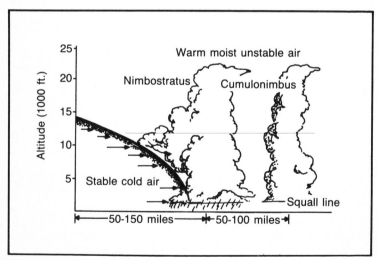

Fig. 5-1. A cold front usually travels about 300 to 400 miles per day in summer, about 500 miles per day in winter.

96

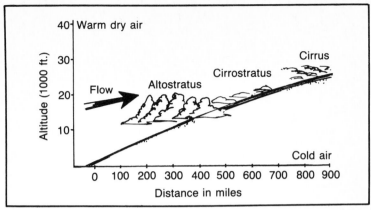

Fig. 5-2. Warm fronts are normally less violent than cold fronts, although they affect a much greater area. The sky generally remains murky after their passage.

warm air (at the height of several thousand feet) will actually be several hundred miles ahead of the front's position on the map.

DEWPOINT

For any given amount of moisture in the air, there is a temperature at which it will condense. That temperature is the *dewpoint.*

Any time temperature and dewpoint approach within 4° of one another, fog, rain, or some other form of precipitation is likely.

LAPSE RATES

Under normal conditions, the temperature of the atmosphere decreases 3½° F per 1000 feet of altitude. This is known as the *normal lapse rate.* Remember this figure; it will come in handy from time to time.

When the Sun's heat sets up a thermal current, the air within this ascending column cools at the rate of 5½° F per 1000 feet until it reaches its dewpoint. This is called the *dry adiabatic lapse rate.* While the air rises, and before it reaches its dewpoint and forms a cloud, its dewpoint decreases 1° F per 1000 feet. So the thermal approaches its dewpoint at the rate of 4½° F per 1000 feet. This figure is useful in determining the height of cumulus clouds that result from thermal activity. We obtain this by simply taking the difference between ground temperature and dewpoint and dividing by 4½.

For example, say the temperature is 87° F on the surface, and the dewpoint is 68° F. The difference is 19 degrees. Dividing 19 by 4½ we get 4.2, so the cloud base is at 4200 feet above ground level.

This method of determining cloud-base altitude is valid only for cumulus-type clouds, but they are often in the weather picture, particularly in warm weather. In practice, this understanding of lapse rates will allow you to determine, before takeoff, how high you must cruise if you are to find smooth air above the thermals. A summer afternoon sky populated with cloud-sheep feeding on thermals gives a very bumpy ride below the cloud base.

CLOUDS

There are only two basic kinds of clouds: *cumulus* and *stratus.* * The many subspecies result from the altitudes at which they are formed and the combining of different kinds. As far as the flier is concerned, it is probably easier and more practical to classify them by altitude:

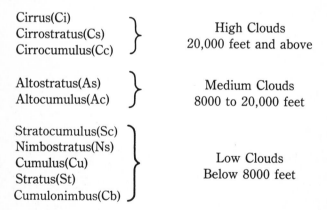

Cirrus(Ci)
Cirrostratus(Cs)
Cirrocumulus(Cc)
} High Clouds
20,000 feet and above

Altostratus(As)
Altocumulus(Ac)
} Medium Clouds
8000 to 20,000 feet

Stratocumulus(Sc)
Nimbostratus(Ns)
Cumulus(Cu)
Stratus(St)
Cumulonimbus(Cb)
} Low Clouds
Below 8000 feet

Cumulonimbus (usually referred to as "Cb's," the weatherman's abbreviation for them) are formed from the ordinary and innocent little cumulus, when the air is unstable. The fluffy cumulus simply begin to build up vertically—often to heights above 30,000 feet— from their low bases.

---

*Many instructors prefer to regard cirrus clouds as a third basic kind. Perhaps it all depends upon how one chooses to explain things.

The common name is "thunderhead," and these towering, castle-like beauties are full of turbulence, violent vertical winds, lightning, and hail; they are extremely dangerous to aircraft. They are classified as low clouds because their bases are low, but you'll never get enough altitude to climb above a mature Cb in a lightplane, so stay away from it. Never fly beneath it, for there are strong air currents feeding it from below, and strong downcurrents spilling down its sides.

Stratus is an even or uniform layer of low fog or heavy haze not touching the ground.

Cumulus we've already discussed. "Cumulus" means "heap," a good descriptive term for the fair-weather type which is white and fluffy and forms at the top of a thermal current.

Nimbostratus is a low, dense, and dark cloud layer from which steady rain or snow usually falls. It is ragged in appearance, and in most cases, altostratus, from which it has formed and settled, lies above.

Stratocumulus forms in rolls and waves. It is low and dangerous for the flier because it presents icing hazards if the temperature is near freezing. Usually, it is not associated with rain, although mist or drizzle is possible.

Altocumulus is somewhat like cirrocumulus in appearance, but the globules or ripples are bigger and more pronounced (Fig. 5-3).

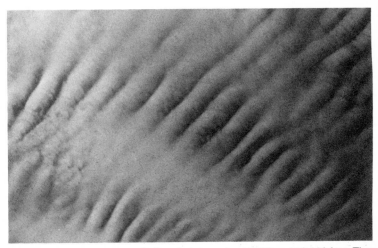

Fig. 5-3. Altocumulus generally form between about 8000 and 18,000 feet. The type shown here signals caution. It often precedes a progressively lower ceiling and some form of precipitation.

It is often called "mackerel sky" and indicates brewing storm conditions.

Altostratus is a dense, grayish sheet, similar to cirrostratus, but heavier and lower. It is ordinarily followed by rain or snow.

Cirrocumulus are small, high-altitude cumulus clouds with a fine grain or ripple pattern. Like altocumulus, they foretell stormy weather (Fig. 5-4).

Cirrostratus gives the sky a milky look. It is a thin, high haze made up of ice crystals, which often causes a ring of light to appear around the Sun or moon. It usually indicates bad weather within 24-36 hours.

Cirrus clouds are the highest of all, and are made of ice crystals. Commonly called "mare's tails" or "feathers," cirrus are carried by very strong upper winds, and often come from the anvil-shaped tops of distant thunderheads.

THE WEATHER MAP

The heavy, curvy lines on the typical surface weather map are lines of equal pressure. They are called *isobars*. Usually, they are drawn 4 *millibars* apart (a millibar is the unit of pressure that meteorologists use instead of inches of mercury, 4 millibars being equal to ⅑ of an inch of mercury. Normal, sea level air pressure

Fig. 5-4. Cirrocumulus form at about 20,000 feet and are made of ice crystals or supercooled water droplets.

of 29.92" Hg is equal to 1013.2 millibars. Because differences in air pressure cause winds, it follows that the closer together the isobars are drawn, the stronger the winds.

Around lows, the wind direction is counterclockwise and, due to surface friction, inward across the isobars at about a 30-degree angle up to 2000 feet above the surface. Above that, the winds will tend to parallel the isobars. Around highs, the wind blows clockwise and outward at about the same angle.

Cold fronts are shown by means of a heavy line with a sawtoothed edge indicating direction of movement. They travel about 300 to 400 miles per day in summer, about 500 miles per day in winter.

Warm fronts are drawn with little half-moons along the side of the line in their direction of movement.

Due to the general wind circulation throughout the world, the United States has prevailing westerly winds (increasingly so with altitude); more often than not—particularly in summer—you can predict tomorrow's weather simply by noting the weather 400 miles west of you today.

Each U.S. Weather Reporting Station is shown on the weather map by means of a coded "station model." Pictured in Fig. 5-5 is a sample station model; a portion of a weather map showing how these reporting stations appear on it is shown in Fig. 5-6.

MOUNTAIN EFFECTS

On the windward side of a mountain, rapidly moving air dams up because of the obstruction to its flow. This causes an increase in pressure on the windward side, and your altimeter will record a lower altitude than is correct. On the leeward side, the air spills over and washes down, creating a decrease in pressure, and your altimeter will show a higher altitude than you actually have. The danger here is apparent, especially if you're flying in conditions of restricted visibility. Also, the downdrafts created on the leeward side add to the danger.

A good rule is to always fly at least 2000 feet higher than the highest peak near your flight path, particularly during marginal weather.

ICING IN FLIGHT

Under certain conditions, ice may form on the struts, tail, wings, and propeller of your aircraft. It can be one of two kinds: *rime ice*,

101

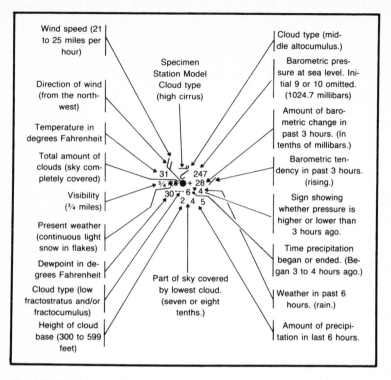

Fig. 5-5. Weather reporting stations shown on the weather map seldom show all of this information.

which resembles the stuff that gathers around the freezer unit of a kitchen refrigerator and flakes off easily; or the hard, clear stuff called *glaze ice*. Glaze ice can easily unbalance the propeller and cause severe engine damage. Either kind may form on the wings, changing the camber and destroying lift.

Icing is likely to be encountered while flying through wet snow, or rain, when the temperature is near freezing or slightly above. It can also form when flying through a cloud layer at near-freezing temperature.

If you should ever find yourself in dangerous icing conditions, either climb to colder air where the moisture is already frozen, or descend to warmer air. But since this advice is not always easy to follow in a lightplane, the safest and sanest bet is to stay clear of probable icing conditions. Call the nearest FSS before taking off into uncertain weather.

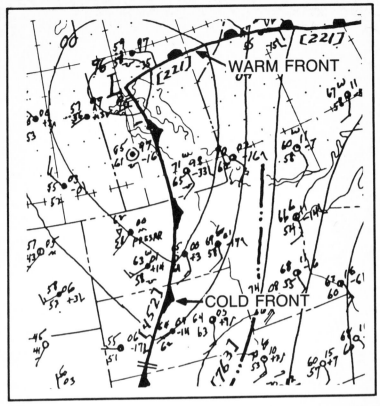

Fig. 5-6. Typical surface weather map showing data sent by various reporting stations.

THE WEATHER DECISION

Now you can easily identify the weather impediments to safe flight. They are lack of visibility, airframe icing, and turbulence. Separately, or together in storms, these are the three conditions produced by weather that threaten us when we fly.

What you must do as a pilot is learn to accurately gauge the extent of these dangers when you see them, and understand the forces which produce them.

Most pilots have long depended upon the Flight Service Station briefer to interpret the current and expected conditions along planned cross-country routes. But the best weather briefing has its limitations, and in any case, the FAA says it will steadily reduce this service in favor of electronic displays that will offer information,

LOCATION IDENTIFIER TYPE AND TIME OF REPORT*	SKY AND CEILING	VISIBILITY WEATHER AND OBSTRUCTION TO VISION	SEA-LEVEL PRESSURE	TEMPERATURE AND DEW POINT	WIND	ALTIMETER SETTING	REMARKS AND CODED DATA
MKC SA 0758	15 SCT M25 OVC	1R-K	132	/58/56	/1807	/993/	RF4LVR2V4

SKY AND CEILING

Sky cover contractions are in ascending order. Figures preceding contractions are heights in hundreds of feet above station. Sky cover contractions are:
CLR Clear: Less than 0.1 sky cover.
SCT Scattered: 0.1 to 0.5 sky cover.
BKN Broken: 0.6 to 0.9 sky cover.
OVC Overcast: More than 0.9 sky cover.
—Thin (When prefixed to SCT, BKN, OVC)
—X Partial obscuration: 0.9 or less of sky hidden by precipitation or obstructon to vision (bases at surface.)
X Obscuration: 1.0 sky hidden by precipitation or obstruction to vision (bases at surface).
Letter preceding height of layer identifies ceiling layer and indicates how ceiling height was obtained. Thus:
E Estimated
M Measured
W Indefinite
V=Immediately following numerical value. indicates a variable ceiling.

VISIBILITY

Reported in statute miles and fractions. (V=Variable)

WEATHER AND OBSTRUCTION TO VISION SYMBOLS

A Hail	IC Ice crystals	S Snow
BD Blowing dust	IF Ice fog	SG Snow grains
BN Blowing sand	IP Ice pellets	SP Snow pellets
BS Blowing snow	IPW Ice pellet showers	SW Snow showers
D Dust	K Smoke	T Thunderstorms
F Fog	L Drizzle	ZL Freezing drizzle
GF Ground fog	R Rain	ZR Freezing rain
H Haze	RW Rain showers	

Precipitation intensities are indicated thus: — Light; (no sign) Moderate; + Heavy

WIND

Direction in tens of degrees from true north, speed in knots; 0000 indicates calm. G indicates gusty. Peak speed of gusts follows G or Q when gusts or squall are reported. The contraction WSHFT followed by GMT time group in remarks indicates windshift and its time of occurrence. (Knots X 1.15=statute mi./hr.)
EXAMPLES: 3627=360 Degrees, 27 knots; 3627G40=360 Degrees, 27 knots, peak speed in gusts 40 knots.

ALTIMETER SETTING
The first figure of the actual altimeter setting is always omitted from the report.

RUNWAY VISUAL RANGE (RVR)
RVR is reported from some stations. Extreme values during 10 minutes prior to observation are given in hundreds of feet. Runway identification precedes RVR report.

PILOT REPORTS (PIREPS)
When available, PIREPS, in fixed-formats are appended to weather observations. The PIREP is desgnated by UA.

DECODED REPORT
Kansas City: Record observation taken at 0758 GMT 1500 feet scattered clouds, measured ceiling 2500 feet overcast, visibility 1 mile, light rain, smoke, sea-level pressure 1013.2 millibars, temperature 58°F, dewpoint 56°F, wind 180°, 7 knots, altimeter setting 29.93 inches. Runway 04 left, visual range 2000 feet variable to 4000 feet.

*TYPE OF REPORT
SA—a scheduled record observation
SP—an unscheduled special observation indicating a significant change in one or more elements
RS—a scheduled record observation that also qualifies as a special observation.
All three types of observations (SA, SP, RS) are followed by a 24 hour-clock-time-group in GMT.

U.S. DEPARTMENT OF COMMERCE — NATIONAL OCEANIC AND ATMOSPHERIC ADMINISTRATION — NATIONAL WEATHER SERVICE

Fig. 5-7. Pilots will find an increasing need to decipher and analyze weather data themselves. Here are the symbols and sequence of teletype weather reports.

but no interpretation or advice. This means that, to an ever-increasing extent, pilots are going to have to rely on their own evaluations of the data reported (Figs. 5-7, 5-8, and 5-9).

You can do it (some have done it for years). It is easier if you understand the limitations of the reporting system and the current state of the art. First of all, situations that *cannot* be predicted with acceptable accuracy are:

- The time that freezing rain will begin.
- Location and occurrence of severe turbulence.
- Location and occurrence of heavy icing.
- Tornadoes.
- Ceilings of 100 feet or less before they occur.
- Thunderstorms which have not visibly begun to form.

Fig. 5-8. You'll need to translate forecasts also.

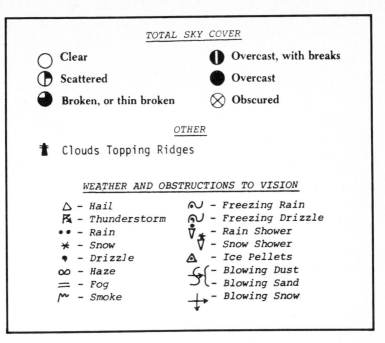

TOTAL SKY COVER

○ Clear

◐ Scattered

◕ Broken, or thin broken

◑ Overcast, with breaks

● Overcast

⊗ Obscured

OTHER

♠ Clouds Topping Ridges

WEATHER AND OBSTRUCTIONS TO VISION

△ – Hail
🆁 – Thunderstorm
•• – Rain
✱ – Snow
❦ – Drizzle
∞ – Haze
= – Fog
/⌐ – Smoke

∿ – Freezing Rain
∿ – Freezing Drizzle
▿ – Rain Shower
▿ – Snow Shower
⬠ – Ice Pellets
⤦ – Blowing Dust
⤦ – Blowing Sand
⤓ – Blowing Snow

Fig. 5-9. These aren't Egyptian hieroglyphics. They're just the symbols used on aviation weather depiction charts.

- Fog.
- The position of a hurricane center more than 12 hours in advance.

In short, the worse it is, the less the weather people know about it in advance. This underscores the pilot's need to make on-the-spot weather decisions for himself (Fig. 5-10).

Here are the accuracy factors and limitations applying to situations that weather specialists can forecast usefully:

- A forecast of good flying weather (ceiling 3000 feet or more and visibility 3 miles or greater) is usually dependable up to 12 hours in advance.
- A forecast of poor flying weather (ceiling below 1000 feet and visibility less than 1 mile) is much less accurate 12 hours in advance, but is 80 percent accurate for a three- to four-hour period.
- Ceiling and visibility reports should be highly suspect beyond the first two or three hours of the forecast period.

105

Fig. 5-10. Again, your need to "get there" should never influence your assessment of the weather.

- Forecasts of poor flying conditions are most reliable when there is a distinct weather system such as a front, trough, precipitation, etc., although there is a general tendency among weathermen to forecast these on the optimistic side.
- Weather associated with fast-moving cold fronts and squall lines is the most difficult to accurately forecast.
- Surface visibility forecasts are less reliable than predicted ceilings.
- Snow reduces visibility forecasts to pure guesswork.

It is evident from the above FAA study that the weather most likely to give you trouble is the hardest to predict.

You can take some useful guidelines from the above if you apply the weather basics discussed earlier. Prepare for a cross-country flight by including the following:

- Check locations of low pressure areas, fronts, and troughs. Fast-moving cold fronts usually mean quick violence (particularly, if they are moving in on an area of warm, moist air), quick clearing, and bumpy air. Slow-moving cold fronts may have much the same weather associated with them as warm fronts, with wide frontal zones of poor visibility, precipitation, turbulence, and icing above the freezing level. Not all fronts are severe; the amount of moisture present, is the determining factor.

- Check moisture content and stability of the airmass through which you plan to fly. Temperature-dewpoint spreads reveal moisture content, and unstable or conditionally unstable air allows thunderhead build-up.
- Check winds aloft and note the freezing level. These factors, plus visibility considerations, the altitude separation rule, and perhaps, a desire to get above convective turbulence, all contribute to the selection of your cruising altitude.
- When thunderstorms are present, request altitudes of bases and tops. Building thunderheads will have strong updrafts below their bases. Do not fly closer than five miles downwind of an overhanging anvil; hail sometimes is thrown from the top of a thunderhead. Never fly beneath mountain thunderstorms even if the area on the other side of the mountains can be seen.
- The danger of structural icing exists in a moist airmass at temperatures below freezing, particularly within cumuliform clouds. Hard glaze ice is common in cumuliform clouds. Rime ice is common in stratiform clouds.
- Carburetor ice may form at temperatures as high as $25°$ C in moist air. It is most likely when the temperature and dewpoint approach $20°$ C. Air intake ducts to the engine are most susceptible to icing when temperature and dewpoint are near $10°$ C or lower.
- Approach mountain ridges at an angle when possible, and predetermine the wind direction. If clouds are present, they will usually be over the lee side. If winds are strong, climb to at least 2000 feet above the ridge before reaching it. Winds in excess of 50 kts. may create a standing wave over the lee side of high mountains. The turbulence may extend for many miles. Lenticular clouds indicate standing waves, but will not form if the airmass is dry.
- Beware of *wind shear* associated with temperature inversions at low altitudes during landing and takeoff operations. Wind shear occurs when two adjacent airmasses are moving in different directions. Transition from one to the other will temporarily affect your airspeed. The inversions are often the result of a mass of relatively warm air moving over a cooler surface air mass, which is sometimes trapped by terrain such as a valley.
- A clearance from a ground controller to change altitudes in flight, to approach and land, or in fact, to do anything at all,

means *only* that it is safe to do so insofar as other air traffic is concerned. The controller's primary responsibility is safe separation of air traffic, and all he may know about you, in most cases, is where you are, your direction of flight, and the kind of airplane you are flying.

As pilot-in-command, it is *your* responsibility to conduct a flight within the limits of your ability. If a controller should direct you into a weather situation that you do not feel you can safely handle, you have the legal right to refuse that directive (explain your refusal to the controller, of course).

If you find yourself in a pressure situation, perhaps approaching a busy airport for the first time, *tell* the controller that you are a student pilot. It helps.

Chapter 6
VFR Navigation
and Communications

IN THE UNITED STATES, all aircraft fly under either Visual Flight Rules (VFR) or Instrument Flight Rules (IFR), depending primarily on weather conditions, aircraft equipment, pilot qualifications, and pilot preference. As a student pilot or newly licensed private pilot, you'll strictly be flying under VFR.

VFR WEATHER MINIMUMS

There are minimum weather conditions in which you can fly VFR. These visibility and distance-from-clouds rules are shown in Table 6-1. Actually, the cloud separation rules are one of the gray areas of flying. Without a reference of some kind, it is difficult, if not impossible, to judge your distance from a cloud.

If weather conditions are worse than these minimums, you must fly IFR, but you can do so only after you have obtained an instrument rating.

RIGHT-OF-WAY RULES

Because you won't be flying in the clouds, it will be your responsibility to "see and avoid" other aircraft.

Like the rules governing an automobile's right-of-way at an intersection, rules have been established (FAR 91.67) to prevent mid-air collisions. You need to remember them, because you won't

Table 6-1. VFR Visibility and Cloud Separation Minimums.

ALTITUDE	UNCONTROLLED AIRSPACE		CONTROLLED AIRSPACE	
	Flight Visibility	Distance From Clouds	**Flight Visibility	**Distance From Clouds
1200' or less above the surface, regardless of MSL Altitude.	*1 statute mile	Clear of clouds	3 statute miles	500' below 1000' above 2000' horizontal
More than 1200' above the surface, but less than 10,000' MSL.	1 statute mile	500' below 1000' above 2000' horizontal	3 statute miles	500' below 1000' above 2000' horizontal
More than 1200' above the surface and at or above 10,000' MSL.	5 statute miles	1000' below 1000' above 1 statute mile horizontal	5 statute miles	1000' below 1000' above 1 statute mile horizontal

*Helicopters may operate with less than 1 mile visibility, outside controlled airspace at 1200 feet or less above the surface, provided they are operated at a speed that allows the pilot adequate opportunity to see any air traffic or obstructions in time to avoid collisions.

**In addition, when operating within a control zone beneath a ceiling, the ceiling must not be less than 1000'. If the pilot intends to land or takeoff or enter a traffic pattern within a control zone, the ground visibility must be at least 3 miles at that airport. If ground visibility is not reported at the airport, 3 miles flight visibility is required. (FAR 91.105)

have time to look them up when you discover a 747 playing "chicken" with you at 10,000 feet. Here are the current rules:

* *

FAR 91.67: Right-of-way rules; except water operations.

(a) General. When weather conditions permit, regardless of whether an operation is conducted under Instrument Flight Rules or Visual Flight Rules, vigilance shall be maintained by each person operating an aircraft so as to see and avoid other aircraft in compliance with this section. When a rule of this section gives another aircraft the right-of-way, he shall give way to that aircraft and may not pass over, under, or ahead of it, unless well clear.

(b) In distress. An aircraft in distress has the right-of-way over all other air traffic.

(c) Converging. When aircraft of the same category are converging at approximately the same altitude (except head-on or nearly so), the aircraft to the other's right has the right-of-way. If the aircraft are of different categories—

   (1) A balloon has the right-of-way over any other category of aircraft;

   (2) A glider has the right-of-way over an airship, airplane, or rotorcraft; and

   (3) An airship has the right-of-way over an airplane or rotorcraft.

      However, an aircraft towing or refueling other aircraft

has the right-of-way over all other engine-driven aircraft.

(d) Approaching head-on. When aircraft are approaching each other head-on, or nearly so, each pilot of each aircraft shall alter course to the right.

(e) Overtaking. Each aircraft that is being overtaken has the right-of-way, and each pilot of an overtaking aircraft shall alter course to the right to pass well clear.

(f) Landing. Aircraft, while on final approach to land, or while landing, have the right-of-way over other aircraft in flight or operating on the surface. When two or more aircraft are approaching an airport for the purpose of landing, the aircraft at the lower altitude has the right-of-way, but it shall not take advantage of this rule to cut in front of another which is on final approach to land, or to overtake that aircraft.

(g) Inapplicability. This section does not apply to the operation of an aircraft on water.

* *

As you can see, most of it is simply a matter of common sense and courtesy. In practice, regardless of the rules, you'll be wise to always give airliners and military aircraft plenty of room and assume that their pilots don't see you. To a large degree, they can't, because of the restricted vision from their machines.

NAVIGATION

Once you've learned the machine and the rules, flying your airplane across country, on an accurate course, is a relatively simple matter. The radio navigation stations that almost unfailingly lead you from anywhere to anywhere in the United States (and much of the rest of the world) have made air navigation so painless that the average private pilot today routinely completes aerial journeys that were, only a few years ago, largely reserved for skilled professionals (Fig. 6-1).

This doesn't mean, however, that all you have to do is learn to tune your avionics (aircraft radios). The FAA has wisely seen to it—via your pilot's license examination—that you will not be a slave to your magical black boxes. So you are required to demonstrate your ability to plot a course and fly it, without regard to your radio navigational aids. If your radios fail, you must be able to navigate on your own.

Fig. 6-1. Cross-country: Point your airplane in any direction; it's a freedom-expander and a distance-shrinker. And the decisions are all your own.

It's significant that the FAA regards its multi-zillion dollar airways system as an *aid* to air navigation; it's there simply to make things easier, more efficient and safer. It doesn't relieve you of your responsibility to *plan* and *think*.

"Contact" air navigation is not hard. A ruler with a protractor attached to it—called a *plotter*—is the only item of equipment you need, other than aeronautical charts. The clock and compass in the plane do the rest, although a pocket computer can make it easier (Fig. 6-2).

Aeronautical Charts

You'll spend a lot of time studying the *Sectional* and/or *World Aeronautical Charts* (WACs) put out by the National Ocean Service. The information contained in these charts is amazing, and the reverse side of each chart offers the symbols and explanations needed for its interpretation. (Fig. 6-3).

The Sectional is drawn 8-miles-to-the-inch, and the World Aeronautical is 16-miles-to-the-inch, so the popular (with lightplane pilots) Sectional is more detailed, while the WAC covers a larger area. The Sectional covers an area approximately 150 by 285 miles;

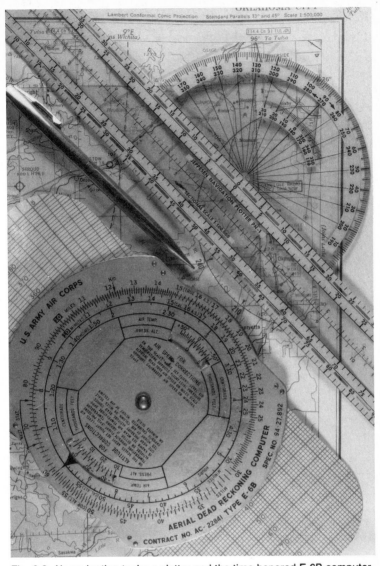

Fig. 6-2. Air navigation tools: a plotter and the time-honored E-6B computer. Today, the E-6B and its clones are rapidly being supplanted by electronic pocket models.

the WAC an area of about 285 by 400 miles. It takes 37 sectionals to cover the conterminous U.S.; each is identified by a major city it serves.

Ground elevation is indicated by a color code ranging from

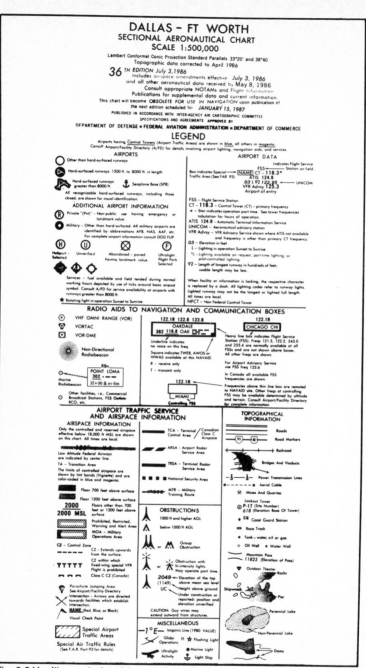

Fig. 6-3 You'll spend a lot of time studying Sectionals. They contain an amazing amount of information.

green at sea level through successively darker shades of brown as terrain height increases.

You'll notice, too, that beneath the name of each airport is a code showing the facilities available. For example, Wichita (Kansas) Mid-Continent Airport is listed this way:

FSS
WICHITA
MID-CONTINENT
CT-**118.2** ATIS **125.5**
1332 L 103 **122.95**

This means there is an FAA Flight Service Station with all of its many aids and comforts; control tower and primary radio frequency is 118.2 on your radio; Automatic Terminal Information Service is on 125.5; field elevation is 1332 feet above sea level; runways are lighted; the longest runway is 10,300 feet in length; and aeronautical advisories are transmitted in 122.95 (UNICOM). You'll also note that runways are shown, outlined in heavy blue ink so that you get a clear mental picture of the airport layout.

And there's much more on the charts: the limits of control areas, other radio frequencies, heights of obstructions, restricted areas, etc.

Do not fly anywhere cross-country without the appropriate, *current* aeronautical charts. These essential accoutrements sell for about $3.75 each at your local airport (in the mid-1960s the price was 30¢—ah, inflation!) A plastic plotter costs about $4.00, unless your FBO is without competition. (In fairness, FBOs are not greedy by nature. If their prices sometimes seem high, it's usually because the local municipal government is extracting the maximum possible rent—often including a percentage of fuel sales—from them, and because of such invisible expenses as liability insurance premiums.)

If your local FBO lacks a decent selection of pilot supplies, you might want to try Sporty's Pilot Shop (Clermont County Airport, Batavia, OH 45103). Every aviation person should be on the Sporty's mailing list. It's probably the fastest source for up-to-date charts and other av-things you'll need (or think you'll need). Their catalog is free for the asking.

Meridians and Parallels

You are probably familiar with the imaginary lines around the

Earth which navigators use in determining position and direction. The parallel lines that start at the equator and are equidistant up to the North Pole (and down to the South Pole) are called *parallels of latitude.* These determine points on the globe in a north-south direction.

Meridians are lines of *longitude,* which run from one pole to the other. That is, they converge at the poles, although they are a good distance apart at the equator. These are used to measure east-west direction, and as a reference in obtaining a *true course.*

The meridian that passes through Greenwich, England, is (by international agreement) the *prime* or *zero* meridian. Locations west of it, around to the 180th meridian (the halfway point), have west longitude, while locations around the other way, to the 180th, have east longitude.

Obtaining a Course

True course (TC) is the direction, measured in degrees, in which your destination lies with relation to the geographic North Pole. Imagine yourself facing north and standing in the center of a circle which is marked off around its rim in 360 equal parts. If 0° is north, then 90° is east; 180°, south; and 270°, west. 360° coincides with 0° at north.

In Fig. 6-4 we are determining a true course, using the Dallas-Ft. Worth Sectional. We have drawn a line from the Childress (Texas) airport to the Mangum (Oklahoma) airport. For this illustration, assume we're in Childress and our destination is Mangum.

After drawing the course line from one airport symbol to the other, our second step is to find the *mid-meridian* between us and our destination. OK, that's easy; this is a short trip and there's only one meridian between these two towns.

Next, we place our plotter's straightedge along the course line with the protractor's zero-hole on the mid-meridian. Then we simply read our true course in degrees on the protractor scale where the mid-meridian emerges from it. In this case, it is 053°.

Cruising Altitudes

Before proceeding with further calculations, you must determine the altitude at which you should fly. Under VFR, if you want to cruise more than 3000 feet above the surface (and below 18,000 feet MSL), you are limited to certain altitudes, based on your magnetic course (MC). To determine MC, take your TC and

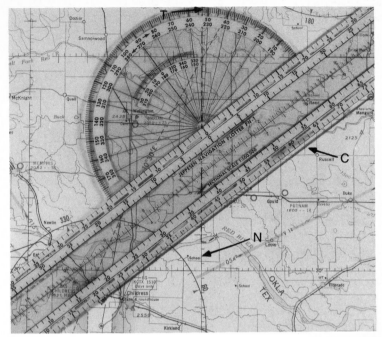

Fig. 6-4. Obtaining a true course: Position your plotter with the protractor's center hole on the mid-meridian (N) and the straightedge along the course line (C). True course, 053°, is then indicated on the protractor's scale (T).

correct it for magnetic variation (which is explained later in this chapter).

If your MC is 0-179° (east), you must fly at an *odd* thousand-foot MSL altitude *plus 500 feet* (e.g., 3500, 5500, 7500, etc.).

If your MC is 180 - 359° (west), you must fly at an *even* thousand-foot MSL altitude *plus 500 feet* (e.g., 4500, 6500, 8500, etc.).

This rule separates eastbound traffic from westbound traffic to prevent head-on conflicts. The specific altitude you decide upon depends on your aircraft's service ceiling, terrain elevation, freezing level, cloud levels, turbulence levels, airspace restrictions, and winds aloft. You'll want an altitude with good tailwinds, if possible, to save you time and fuel. On our Childress—Mangum trip, we'll be headed east, so we'll choose an odd thousand-foot level plus 500 feet.

Wind Correction Angle

Once an airplane is airborne, it will be carried along in the same

117

direction as the air mass that supports it. It will always fly *through* the air at its regular speed, but it will be carried *with* the air, just as a boat is carried with the current, independent of its speed through the water. Just as you must point a boat's nose to one side of its intended destination in order to compensate for sideways drift, so you must do the same with an airplane.

If the wind direction and velocity are known, it's easy to establish the proper amount of correction necessary to follow a given course. It is computed by means of a *wind vector** and works like this:

1) Draw a vertical line on a blank sheet of paper. Mark it with an "N" representing north at the top. It represents your mid-meridian. Place the zero-hole of your plotter on this line, and turn the plotter until your true course, 053°, lines up with the simulated mid-meridian. Then, reproduce your course line from the meridian, along the bottom of the plotter straightedge as shown. This line's length is not important, but its direction corresponds with the course line previously drawn on your chart (Fig. 6-5).

2) Now, for the wind. Let's say the weather people have given it as 30 kts. from 330° at the altitude you'll fly. Line up the plotter with the zero-hole at the point where the course line meets the meridian and, using the inside scale on the protractor for this half of the compass, draw a line representing the wind. This line begins at the meridian and extends in the direction the wind is blowing. Its length is determined by wind velocity, and your wind vector becomes a scale drawing from this point. The most convenient scale is along the straightedge of the plotter. You can use the full wind velocity and airspeed values, or, in order to keep your diagram down in size, you can reduce those values by half. In this example, the 30-kt. wind

---

*It's true that a wind vector is unnecessary when navigating by VOR radio, and that the wind correction angle may be obtained more quickly and easily from the reverse side of your pocket computer. Nevertheless, the wind vector drawing is still considered very valuable in student pilot training by most instructors because it instills a keen "wind sense." It gives you a good mental picture of the drift forces acting upon your plane, and imparts a sure "feel" for corrections that must be ad-libbed on those occasions when you may be temporarily without VOR and wind is not as forecast.

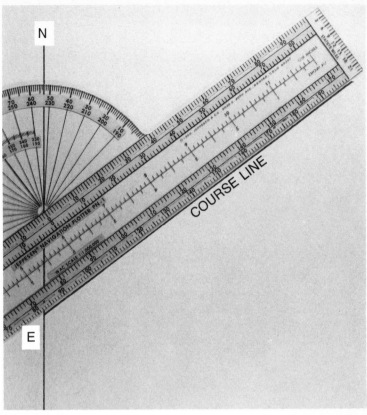

Fig. 6-5. Wind vector, first step: Reproduce your course line of 053° on a blank sheet of paper. The vertical line (N) represents the mid-meridian.

aloft is represented by a line 15 miles long, as measured by the plotter's scale (Fig. 6-6).

3) The final step is to intercept the course line with a line drawn from the outer end of the measured wind line. The length of this final line is determined by your true airspeed (TAS). Let's assume here that your normal TAS at the altitude you intend to fly is 115 kts. (Now you can see why it's easier to halve the speed values. That makes this final line only 57 nautical miles long and gives you a more compact figure to draw.)

The completed vector appears in Fig. 6-7. The result: The angle

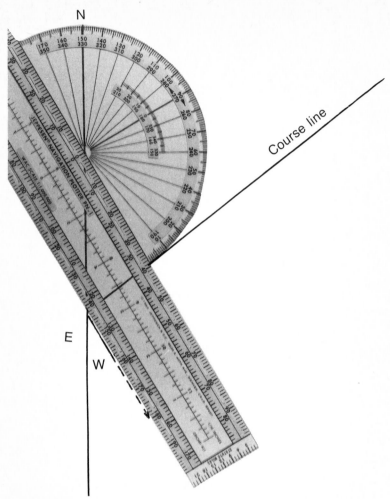

Fig. 6-6. Wind vector, second step: Add the 30-kt. wind from 330°. Line E-W is 15 miles long, representing half of the 30-kt. wind.

at P, measured with your protractor, is the amount of correction necessary for the wind. It is your *wind correction angle* (WCA). And the length of Line E-P is half of your ground speed. Measuring your completed vector, you'll learn that your ground speed is 54 (the length of Line E-P) × 2, or 108 kts., and your WCA is 15°.

This process may seem complicated, but you've actually drawn only four lines. With a little practice, you'll do a wind vector in less than a minute.

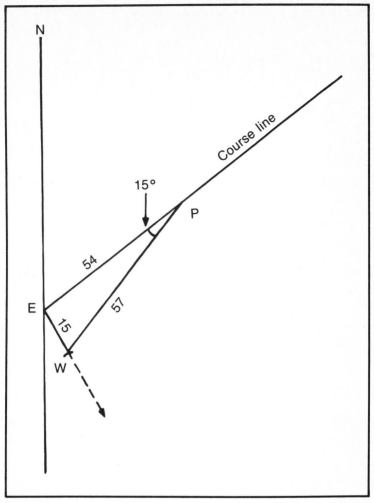

Fig. 6-7. Wind vector, third step: The final line to draw (Line W-P) is the airplane's airspeed (drawn to half-scale). The angle at P is the wind correction angle, 15°. The resulting line, E-P, measures out at 54 miles long. Double that to get your ground speed, 108 kts.

So now that you have a WCA, what do you do with it? Well, you apply it to your true course according to this rule: *Add right— Subtract left.* This means that if the wind is from your right, add 15° to your true course; if the wind is from your left, you'll subtract 15°.

In this case, a glance at your vector shows wind to be from your left. Subtract it to get your *true heading* (TH), 038°. In other words, due to the winds, you'll point your plane's nose at 038° in order to follow a track over the ground of 053°.

Variation and Deviation

Now don't go away; there are a couple more corrections to be made before you arrive at the figure you'll actually follow on the compass.

You take the first one from your aeronautical chart. It's called *variation,* and it's the difference between true north and the actual magnetic lines-of-force radiating from the magnetic pole that attracts the compass. The chart shows—by means of a heavy, red, dashed line—that the area between Childress and Mangum has a magnetic variation of 8° east.

Here's your other navigational rule: *Add west—Subtract east* for magnetic variation. (You might remember this one better by the rhyme, "East is least, and west is best.")

Since your magnetic variation is given as 8° east, subtract it from your true heading of 038°. The result will be your *magnetic heading (MH),* 030°.

Finally, you need to correct for *deviation.* Deviation is error in the compass itself, caused by radio equipment and other disturbing magnetic forces in the airplane. Deviation figures are different for each airplane installation and are always listed on a little card near the compass.

The compass deviation card is mounted directly on the bracket that holds the compass above the windshield in our Cessna 150. The card notes that when flying in a northeasterly direction (such as 030°) you must steer the plane on a *compass heading* of 2° less than your desired magnetic heading. So subtract 2°.

Your final figure then is 028°; this is your compass heading. It is the actual reading you want to see on your magnetic compass in order to make good a true course of 053°.

Here's a recap of the steps:

a) Start with......................True course   053
b) Apply................................WCA   −015
   Result........................True heading   038
c) Apply.............................Variation   −008
   Result.....................Magnetic heading   030
d) Apply.............................Deviation   −002
   Final Result.................Compass heading   028

Remember the two rules: For variation, add west and subtract east. For wind, add right and subtract left.

The magnetic compass will oscillate considerably in rough air, and after a turn, it requires a minute or so to steady down. Therefore, it can't be used *during* a turn as a reference in changing your heading. One of the advantages of having a gyro compass is that it reacts only in relation to the yaw of the airplane and stops swinging when the plane does. But it can't replace your magnetic compass because it does not sense direction on its own and must be manually set by reference to the magnetic compass, when the magnetic compass is at rest.

Maintaining Course by Pilotage

Now, let's plan and fly a different cross-country trip. Start from Wichita and go to Tulsa. First, draw a course line on your chart from the Wichita Mid-Continent Airport symbol to the Tulsa International Airport symbol (Fig. 6-8). Then take your plotter, place it on the mid-meridian and determine true course; it's 140°.

In practice, you'll check with the weather people first and, among other things, they'll give you wind directions and velocities, from the surface up to your aircraft's service ceiling, the highest altitude at which it is designed to fly.

Let's assume you choose to fly this VFR trip at 5500 feet where you expect a wind from 270° at 25 kts. That's not squarely on your tail, but enough so that it will help. You also select a power setting that will give you a true airspeed of 100 kts.

Next, do your wind vector; it should look like Fig. 6-9. The vector reveals that the wind correction angle (measured at P), is 12°. The wind is from your right, so this figure is added to your TC to give you a true heading of 152°.

Variation, taken from the chart, is 7° east for this part of the country. Following the second rule (add west—subtract east), subtract 7° from true heading. This leaves you with a magnetic heading of 145°.

Finally, glance at the compass deviation card in the airplane and find that, in this quadrant of the compass, you must steer a compass heading 2° greater than your magnetic heading. So you end up with a compass heading of 147°.

Your vector also gives your ground speed when you measure Line E-P. This comes out at 115 kts. You're getting a 15-kt. boost from the partial tailwind.

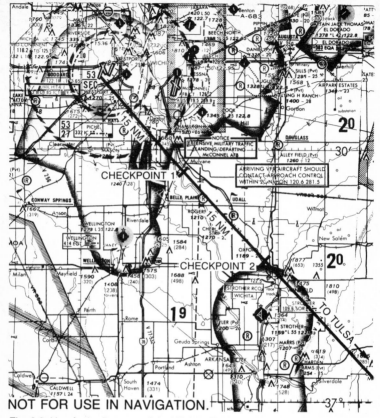

NOT FOR USE IN NAVIGATION.

Fig. 6-8. Here's the first part of the Wichita-Tulsa course line on our chart. The choice of checkpoints is up to you; here, we've put them 15 NM apart.

Measure your course line on the chart, and you'll find that it is 113 nautical miles (NM) to Tulsa. Now you can figure your estimated time en route, either by simple arithmetic, or by use of your pocket computer. For all practical purposes, you can call your ground speed 100 kts., because your reduced speed during climbout from takeoff will easily cut into it that much. At 100 kts. (that's 100 nautical miles per hour), you can expect to arrive at Tulsa in 68 minutes.

To determine that figure, you divide ground speed into the total distance, and multiply the result by 60 in order to obtain the elapsed time in minutes ($113 \div 100 \times 60 = 67.8$). Always add a little time (or subtract a little speed) for climb and descent, depending upon the extent of each.

Next, you need to establish your *checkpoints,* distinctive landmarks along your route that are easy to spot from the air. When you fly by pilotage (navigating visually without using radio aids), checkpoints serve the same purpose that numbered highway signs do for motorists. You'll like to have many of them, no further than 10 or 15 minutes apart, because the "highway" you'll follow is invisible. Select them by arbitrarily placing marks on your course line at, say, 15 NM intervals (when you fly a faster airplane, select checkpoints farther apart). A ground speed of 100 kts. means that you should pass your checkpoints approximately 9 minutes apart, if the wind is as forecast.

As you fly this trip, match up prominent landmarks on the surface with your course line on the chart. For example, the chart shows that, about nine minutes out of Wichita, if you are making good your intended track, you should have crossed the little town of Mulvane—a railroad bridge across a river should be just off your right wing. About 18 minutes out of Wichita, at your second checkpoint, you should be approaching the northwest edge of Winfield, Kansas, easy to identify because the chart shows a race-track and outdoor theater northwest of the town. The many highways and railroad tracks that converge at Winfield also help to identify it from the air. Southeast of Winfield, your second 15-NM checkpoint should put a prominent airport, Strother, about 5 miles ahead and to the right of your track.

Picking your checkpoints is up to you. Another pilot, flying this same trip by pilotage, might make different choices.

Alternate Airport

Occasionally, as a form of insurance, you may decide to turn away from your intended destination because of deteriorating weather, and go to an alternate airport. During the check ride for your license, the FAA inspector may require you to demonstrate your ability to do this.

Let's assume that the Wichita-Tulsa flight is such a check ride and that the inspector suddenly tells you, five minutes after passing your second checkpoint, that weather conditions ahead make it unwise for you to continue to Tulsa.

Your reaction may be: "OK. Can we get back to Wichita?" But the inspector isn't going to make it that easy for you. "No," he claims, "Wichita is now reporting below VFR minimums."

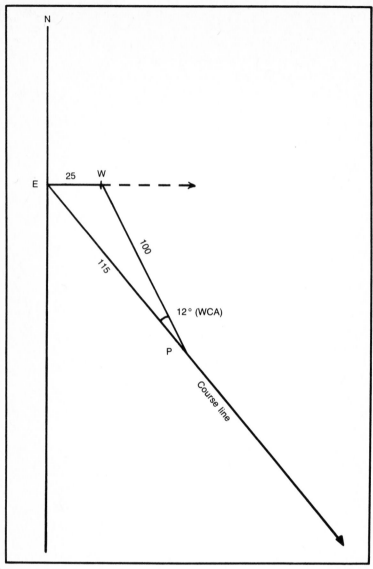

Fig. 6-9. Your Wichita-Tulsa wind vector should look like this, if you do it in full scale.

Well, you've been watching your checkpoints, and you know your ground speed, so you have no trouble pinpointing yourself on the chart. You should be about 8 miles beyond your last checkpoint, and hurriedly placing your plotter's straightedge along your course line, you measure 8 miles from that checkpoint. That should put you almost over a curved highway, running east from Arkansas City. Yes, it's up ahead where it should be.

Now knowing where you are, you check the chart for nearby airport symbols. The closest one shows by its symbol (an "R") that it is a privately owned restricted strip that should only be used by the public in an emergency. But because you flew right by it without seeing it, it can't be much. The next closest public-use airport is Strother, which is now about 5 miles behind and to the right of your current position.

You choose Strother, point to it on the chart (for the inspector's benefit), and turn right, simultaneously coming back on the throttle to begin your descent. You can't actually see the airport yet, but you know where it is relative to Arkansas City and Winfield. "We'll be there in about 4 minutes," you tell the inspector.

Of course, this could happen over sparsely populated or mountainous terrain where the closest airport may be much farther away. In that case, you will quickly draw a new course line from where you are to where you want to go (if you failed to plan an alternate before takeoff). But you'll calculate your new heading by ad-libbing the new wind correction angle, or obtaining it from your computer, because it's impractical to attempt a wind vector drawing in the airplane—especially if the weather is going sour in a hurry and your attention is needed outside. Then you'll follow the new course line with a finger on the chart, dividing your attention between the chart and landmarks below as you match up everything possible to ensure that the new heading is, indeed, taking you where you want to go.

You'll find that it's worth an extra few minutes to plan an alternate before takeoff. (It could also mean the difference between passing and failing your flight test). That way, if trouble does develop, you will already know where to go (after a radio contact inquiring of *their* weather) and how to get there.

Sometimes, the nearest alternates might be 50 miles away or more, and if you don't realize that until near the end of a long hop (with a low fuel supply), those alternates will seem pretty unsatisfying. For this reason, you should consider, in all your flight planning, that an alternate destination might be necessary and that you will need to have enough fuel on board to reach it.

Our Cessna 150 carries 22½ gallons of usable fuel. At normal cruise, it burns slightly less than 6 gallons per hour at this altitude. This is roughly a 3¾-hr supply. But thinking about alternates and/or unfavorable winds not in the forecast, always keep about 45 minutes of fuel in reserve, and assume in all your flight planning that the 150 has only three hours and fifteen minutes of fuel to spend. In practice, this is plenty. Few pilots or passengers normally possess a "range" (between rest rooms) that is much greater, and, anyway, on long flights it's nice to stop every three hours or so to stretch your legs, drink some coffee, and check with the weather people.

RADIO AIDS TO NAVIGATION

For more than 30 years, low-frequency radio beams guided (more or less) American fliers from place to place. The old low-frequency stations sent out just four narrow beams, usually at right angles to one another, and you were either "on the beam" or you weren't—assuming it happened to be pointing in the direction you wanted to go. Because these were low-frequency signals, static was often a problem, especially in stormy weather when you needed them the most. But they served surprisingly well most of the time.

VOR

The modern system is called *VOR* or OMNI (for Very High-Frequency Omnidirectional Range). The VOR signal is very high-frequency (VHF) like TV and radar, and, therefore, almost completely free of static. And, as the name suggests, a VOR sends out signals in *all* directions, so you can tune it in and follow its signal to any point on the compass you choose. Magical black boxes? Undoubtedly.

The VOR receiver in your plane employs three components: a *course selector,* a *course deviation indicator (CDI),* and a *TO-FROM indicator* (Fig. 6-10).

The course selector is a dial that you manually set to the magnetic bearing (to or from the VOR station) on which you wish to fly.

The course deviation indicator is a needle that swings right or left to show your deviation from the bearing you have selected.

The TO-FROM indicator in the little window of the instrument face indicates—naturally—either "TO" or "FROM." But it doesn't tell you whether you are actually approaching or going away from the station to which you are tuned. Rather, it tells you whether the specific course you've dialed in will take you to or from the station—if you fly that course.

Fig. 6-10. A VOR can lead you directly to your destination. Turn your course selector knob (A) to the magnetic heading you wish to fly (B); and tune the proper VOR transmitter (E). Center the deviation needle (C) and keep it centered. If you are flying toward a VOR sttion, you want the "TO-FROM" flag to show "TO". The voice communications side of this magical black box is indicated at V.

Let's take an example again. Let's say that your Wichita-Tulsa flight is to be made by VOR navigation. Referring to the aeronautical chart, note that the Wichita VOR is about 5 miles NW of Wichita Mid-Continent. VOR stations are shown on the chart by means of a blue dot inside a hexagon and surrounded by a compass rose.* Each is identified in a blue rectangular "box" that includes its frequency and coded identifier. In this case, you'll see this box at the bottom of the compass rose: WICHITA, 113.8.

Draw a course line from the Wichita VOR to the Tulsa VOR. It will, in this case, closely follow the course line we previously drew between the airports, though, as you approach Tulsa, it is about 4 miles east of that track, which we flew without radio aids. The course line drawn between the two VOR stations emerges from

---

*Actually, the Wichita VOR is a *VORTAC*, indicated by the three blue "legs" on the hexagon. Although the terms are often used interchangeably, a VORTAC also provides signals for *distance measuring equipment* (DME) and tactical military navigation. You can get a DME receiver to go with your VOR receiver. This brainy little box will keep you informed of your exact air-to-ground distance to or from the VOR station you have tuned. It sends out a signal, and by precisely measuring the milliseconds required for the signal to bounce back, transposes this information into miles, which appear on a digital display on the instrument panel.

the printed compass rose at about 130°. This is a magnetic bearing, with variation already taken into account (Fig. 6-11).

You'll simply take off from Wichita, dial your course selector to 130°, tune in the VOR station on 113.8 MHz, then fly southeast for about 4 miles to intercept the 130° *radial* from the station.

After aligning yourself on course, you merely "fly the needle"—keep it centered, and it'll lead you straight to the Tulsa VOR. The TO-FROM indicator will point to FROM, because if you fly the 130° course you have selected, you will be going away from the station.

Now you know why I call it "magical." Many of us who can remember how it used to be still find it slightly amazing that we can navigate an airplane from Point A to Point B nowadays with utter precision—and almost no effort.

If there is a crosswind, you will discover that holding 130° degrees on the magnetic compass will not usually keep the needle centered. If you find that you must steer 5°, 10°, or even more, to either side of the compass in order to keep the needle centered, do it. The difference between your selected course and whatever it takes to keep the needle centered is simply your wind correction angle. And as long as the needle is centered, you're somewhere along the course you have set on the course selector, regardless of your heading.

To keep your deviation needle centered, "follow it with the plane." In other words, if the needle strays off to the right, turn right to bring it back. It's best to make small corrections.

About halfway to Tulsa, check your chart and you'll find that the frequency of the Tulsa VOR is 114.4 MHz. Therefore, retune your VOR receiver to this frequency. The TO-FROM indicator will switch to TO and, if you are on course, the needle will remain centered.

In practice, there is no need to fly all the way to the Tulsa VOR station itself. Your chart shows it to be about 4 or 5 miles due east of Tulsa International, so you call Tulsa Tower as you overfly Skiatook Airport, and then, as Tulsa International appears in the distance through your right-hand windshield, leave your aerial freeway and go directly to the airport, unless otherwise instructed by the tower.

One more thing about VOR: You need not fly from one VOR station to the next. If both your point of departure and your destination are without nearby VOR sites, you may use those off your course to either side by cross-tuning for frequent position checks. And you can use the *localizer* signal of *instrument landing systems* (ILS) to guide you to airports—in fact, right to the runway. This can be handy in hazy or smoggy conditions, especially when compounded by flying into a setting sun. Just tune the ILS localizer on your VOR receiver, and use the needle to locate the runway centerline.

ADF

Another radio receiver—it's mounted below the VOR Nav/Com set in the center of the panel in our trainer—is the *automatic direction finder* (ADF). Actually, the ADF doesn't find any directions. What it does is bird-dog any low frequency transmitter you tune on it. It will tune commercial radio stations, as well as FAA *non-directional beacons* (NDBs), the latter located on many airports. The ADF needle will point to whichever station you have tuned, and is therefore handy for obtaining en-route position fixes. Or you can follow the signal to its transmitter. In some parts of the world, including much of Latin America, the ADF is the only navaid available.

LORAN-C

The LORAN-C navigation system is becoming increasingly popular with lightplane pilots because it is far more versatile than VOR, provides more information, and does it all for a lot less money.

Originally established more than 40 years ago along U.S. coastlines for long-distance ship navigation, low-frequency LORAN worked well, but the receivers were too heavy and bulky for aircraft use, and the data received had to be plotted by an on-board navigator in order to obtain a useful fix.

The microchip changed all that. The LORAN-C receiver of today, designed specifically for lightplane use, weighs four to six pounds and requires no navigational skills whatever to operate. Lightplane units currently sell for $1000 to $2000.

LORAN-C is very easy to use. In its little microchip brain is a map of the world. Punch in the latitude and longitude of where you are and where you want to go—anywhere at all: a cabin in the north woods, or grandma's south forty. It doesn't have to be an airport.

LORAN will lead you there via a Great Circle route, which is the shortest distance between any two points on a globe. Along the way, you have a constant readout of ground speed, distance remaining to your destination, and a visual course deviation indicator to keep you on track.

Whereas VOR transmitters are normally effective for no more than 100 NM (often less), LORAN is useful for 1000 miles. And because it is low-frequency, it is not limited to line-of-sight as is the VOR signal, but can be received behind mountains and on the ground. The latitude/longitude coordinates of all airports are available in several publications (check with Sporty's); or you can figure your own with the aid of aeronautical charts.

Each LORAN installation consists of a master transmitter and at least two slave transmitters set up several hundred miles apart. The master has a unique pulse and phase signal to distinguish it from its secondaries. The LORAN-C receiver in the airplane measures the time difference (in microseconds) between the arrival of these signals in order to obtain a very accurate fix on the airplane's position. Figure 6-12 illustrates how the three signals

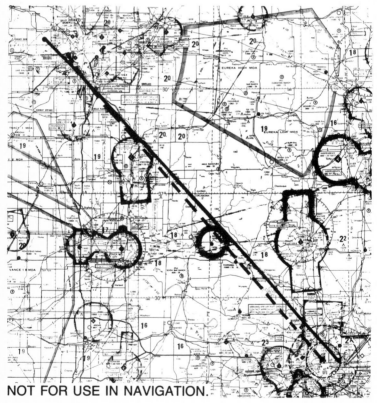

NOT FOR USE IN NAVIGATION.

Fig. 6-11. The dashed line is the track you would fly using pilotage. The solid line is the track between the VOR stations. VORs are not always located as conveniently as these two are.

intersect to achieve this. The principle is a simple (and old) one; the amazing stuff occurs in your on-board computer.

NAVSTAR

NAVSTAR is the air navigation system, based on signals from Earth satellites, that is supposed to replace VOR around 1990 or so. As lightplane pilots we don't especially need it, but the military and airlines want it. So, like the use of "knots" and nautical miles and runways that go halfway to Dallas, we are sure to get it.

CONTROLLED AIRSPACE

Unless you live in a remote desert village or plan to buzz around at treetop level all the time (it's usually illegal), you'll be doing most of your flying within *controlled airspace*. This doesn't mean that you, a VFR flier, will always be controlled by someone on the ground; it just means that, in the airspace you're using, there might be other pilots who *are* being controlled.

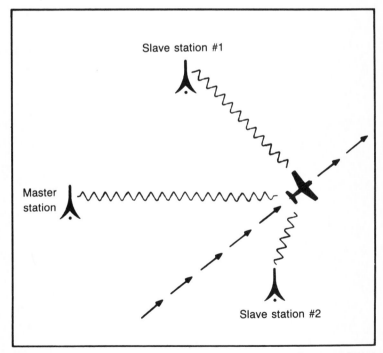

Fig. 6-12. LORAN-C: Signals received from three transmitters allow your LORAN receiver to compute an exact position.

There are several different types of controlled airspace; some overlap (Fig. 6-13). Most of the types you'll be concerned with are depicted on the aeronautical charts for the area in which you'll be flying. Here, summarized, are the types:

- The *Positive Control Area* is airspace (specified in FAR 71.193) within the conterminous U.S. from 18,000 feet to and including Flight Level (FL) 600 (60,000 feet). Except for exam purposes, you won't have to worry too much about this right now, unless you're doing your training in an F-15.

- The *Continental Control Area* consists of the airspace of the 48 contiguous states, the District of Columbia, and Alaska, at and above 14,500 feet MSL, but does not include (1) airspace less than 1500 feet above the surface; or (2) most prohibited and restricted areas.

- *Control Areas* consist of the airspace designated as colored federal airways, VOR federal airways, additional control areas, and control area extensions, but do not include the Continental Control Area. The centerlines of low-altitude VOR federal airways are depicted on your charts as blue lines, but the control areas normally extend 4 nautical miles to either side of the lines.

- *Transition Areas* are designated to contain IFR operations in controlled airspace during approaches and departures. On the charts they are depicted by magenta-tinted, keyhole-shaped areas surrounding airports.

- *Control Zones* extend upward from the surface and terminate at the base of the Continental Control Area. They are normally circular areas with a radius of 5 statute miles around the primary airport (sometimes more than one airport is included), and may also include extensions necessary to include instrument arrival and departure paths. They are depicted as broken blue lines, in the shape of circles or keyholes surrounding airports. Control zones have stricter VFR weather minimums than shown in Table 6-1.

- *Terminal Control Area* (TCA) consists of controlled airspace within which *all* aircraft are subject to strict operating rules for pilots and minimum equipment requirements for aircraft. FAR 91.24 and 91.90 spell out the requirements.

Each TCA location is designated as either a Group I or Group II TCA, and includes at least one primary airport around which the TCA is located. Group I TCAs apply at some of the busiest airports. As a student pilot, you are not allowed to enter a Group I TCA. Group II TCAs are less busy and the requirements are not as stringent as Group I locations.

Currently, there are 23 TCAs. Although they are identified on Sectional charts, if you will be flying regularly in the vicinity of a TCA, you should obtain the appropriate *Terminal Area Chart,* a larger-scale, detailed depiction of the TCA. You will know the TCA rules in detail by the time you have had enough experience to enter these high density traffic areas.

- Airport Radar Service Areas (ARSAs), presently in operation at more than 65 major airports, were recently established to help diminish the chances of mid-air collisions. All aircraft within an ARSA must be in radio contact with air traffic control, although VFR aircraft are not necessarily *controlled.*

  The object of an ARSA is to identify all air traffic, its location and altitude, by ground-based radar so that controllers can direct aircraft to take evasive action whenever a flight path conflict appears to be developing. ARSAs are identified on your Sectional charts. The basic design of an ARSA is shown in Fig. 6-14. Operating rules are found in the *Airman's Information Manual.*

  ARSAs appear to be another of those good ideas that, to date, don't work well in practice.

- Airport Traffic Areas (ATAs) exist at all airports where (and when) a control tower is in operation. An ATA encompasses a 5-nautical-mile circle around the airport and the air above it up to, but not including, 3,000 feet above ground level (AGL). All aircraft taking off, landing, or passing through an ATA, must be in radio contact with the control tower.

There are also various types of *Special Use Airspace,* such as *Prohibited Areas, Restricted Areas,* and *Military Operations Areas.* You'll learn the details of these in your ground-school course.

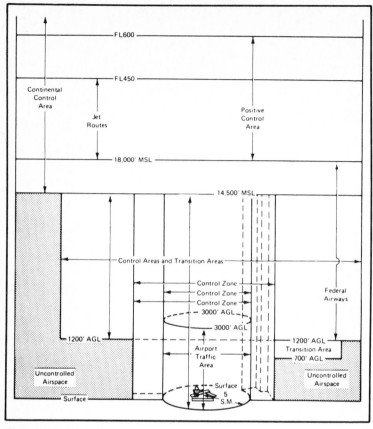

Fig. 6-13. Controlled and uncontrolled airspace above the contiguous 48 United States.

AIR-TO-GROUND COMMUNICATIONS

Before you start talking over your radio to air traffic control, you must learn the modern phonetic alphabet used by controllers:

A—Alpha	J—Juliet	S—Sierra
B—Bravo	K—Kilo	T—Tango
C—Charlie	L—Lima	U—Uniform
D—Delta	M—Mike	V—Victor
E—Echo	N—November	W—Whiskey
F—Foxtrot	O—Oscar	X—X-ray
G—Golf	P—Papa	Y—Yankee
H—Hotel	Q—Quebec	Z—Zulu
I—India	R—Romeo	

Occasionally, you may still hear a Gray Eagle-type employing the old Able-Baker alphabet (possibly because of a typically human urge to let everyone know he was flying airplanes before they were), but there aren't many controllers left who remember it, and they will usually reply in Alpha-Bravo terms.

Also, for clarity, the number nine is pronounced "niner" over the radio.

Tower Talk

To give you the clearest idea of what goes on between you and the control tower people, we'll take another "for instance." Say we're taking off again from Wichita, and going to Tulsa. After we start the engine and are ready to leave, but *before* moving the airplane, we'll call Ground Control (on 121.7 MHz) and the conversation goes like this:

Us: "Wichita Ground Control, this is Cessna Five Niner Three Seven Juliet. At Yingling Aircraft Hangar; ready to taxi. VFR to Tulsa." (Our airplane registration number/call sign is 5937J.)

Tower: "Cessna Three Seven Juliet*, taxi to runway Three Five. Wind, three six zero degrees at seven. Altimeter, two niner niner seven. Hold west of the runway." (He told us to use the runway pointing 350°—runways are numbered according to their magnetic bearing, minus the last digit. Wind is from 360° at 7 knots. Our altimeter setting is 29.97. He also said to stop on the taxi strip west of the runway and wait. He might have had other taxi instructions, particularly if it had been necessary for us to cross a runway in order to reach the assigned runway—never taxi on *any* runway without permission. And if you are not recognized as a "regular" on this field, Ground Control will usually give you the tower frequency. Just remember to follow all instructions and acknowledge all instructions. If you are given an instruction you do not understand, ask the tower to repeat it. If you still don't get it, tell him you are a student pilot; you'll be surprised how much that will simplify things.

We will acknowledge Ground Control's taxi instructions with "Three Seven Juliet." Then, after we've taxied to the position indicated, made our pre-takeoff checks, and are ready to go, we'll switch to the tower frequency (118.2 MHz), listen for a couple of

---

*When a controller abbreviates your call sign, you may use that abbreviation during further communications with the *same* controller.

seconds to make sure no one else is talking, then key our mike button.

Us: "Wichita Tower, Cessna Five Niner Three Seven Juliet. Ready for takeoff."

Tower: "Cessna Three Seven Juliet, cleared for takeoff."

That's all there is to it. Just keep it brief and simple. Also, keep monitoring the tower frequency until you are out of the Airport Traffic Area, just in case they have other traffic information to give you. Remember to always listen on each frequency and wait for a proper break in the chatter before calling in yourself; your aircraft radio is on a pretty sizable party line. Hold your microphone so that it barely touches your upper lip and speak in a normal tone of voice.

Almost all tower people are nice (many are pilots), but they don't have time to chat. On the other hand, never hesitate to ask for clarification of an instruction if you do not completely understand it or because the phraseology is new to you. They understand plain English, and must communicate with you for your safety and the safety of others. In fact, it's just a real good idea to identify yourself as a student pilot on your initial contact with the tower each time. Then the tower will take extra good care of you and give you all the time and leeway you need. At some time during your student period you should telephone the tower and tell them you'd like to come up for a visit *at their convenience*. Some instructors insist on this. You'll spend a pleasant hour or so, you'll learn a lot, and you'll be a better pilot for it (Fig. 6-15).

A few miles out of Tulsa—say, 10 or 15, and certainly before you enter the ARSA—you'll check your chart for the radio frequency at Tulsa Tower, call them, identify yourself, and give your approximate position.

Us: "Tulsa Tower, Cessna Five Niner Three Seven Juliet. Over Skiatook (a little town you have identified below) at two thousand five hundred. Landing Tulsa. Over."

Tower: "Cessna Three Seven Juliet, Tulsa Tower. Left turn, runway Three Six. Wind, three three zero degrees at five. Altimeter, three zero zero five."

Us: "Three Seven Juliet."

We will enter the left-hand traffic pattern at 800 feet AGL, and then will receive clearance to land if there are no other planes immediately ahead of us. At large airports, we can expect to be directed to the proper exit taxiway and given the ground control frequency after landing.

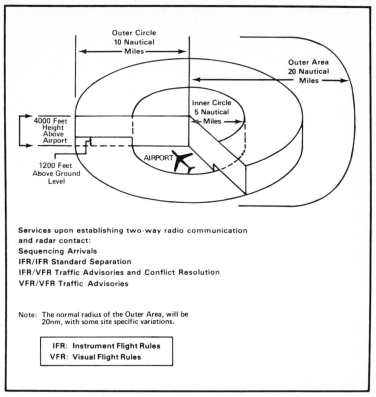

Fig. 6-14. Airport Radar Service Area (ARSA). Establish radio contact with ATC before flying through.

Light Signals

What happens if the radio fails?

Every tower still keeps a signaling device, called a "biscuit gun," with which the controller can aim a steady or flashing colored light beam at you to maintain a minimum of communications. The meaning of those signals are found in Table 6-2.

At night, acknowledge these signals by blinking your landing lights. It's unnecessary to waggle your wings in response during daylight hours, and anyway, the controller can't waggle the tower in reply.

A large white "X" displayed in the center of a field indicates that the field is closed. A similar symbol on any runway means that runway is closed.

Fig. 6-15. Air traffic in the vicinity of an airport, and on the runways and taxiways, is controlled by the men and women in the tower. Before you complete your pilot training, phone them and ask to go up there for a visit (at their convenience). It will be a pleasant and instructive experience.

Common Traffic Advisory Frequencies

The FAA's Airport/Facility Directory lists *Common Traffic Advisory Frequencies* (CTAFs) for advising the world in general of your intentions when operating to or from an airport with no control tower, a tower that is closed, or an FSS that is closed.

UNICOM. UNICOM is a private radio operation, owned by an FBO for the convenience of its customers. It provides a communications channel (often 122.8 MHz) between pilots and an airport, especially an airport without a control tower. When available at a field with a tower, the UNICOM frequency is 122.95 MHz. Both the ground station and the aircraft transmit and receive on the same frequency.

There are many uses for UNICOM, not the least of which is transmitting your intentions when approaching or departing an

Table 6-2. Light Gun Signals.

COLOR AND TYPE OF SIGNAL	MEANING		
	MOVEMENT OF VEHICLES EQUIPMENT AND PERSONNEL	AIRCRAFT ON THE GROUND	AIRCRAFT IN FLIGHT
Steady green	Cleared to cross, proceed or go	Cleared for takeoff	Cleared to land
Flashing green	Not applicable	Cleared for taxi	Return for landing (to be followed by steady green at the proper time)
Steady red	STOP	STOP	Give way to other aircraft and continue circling
Flashing red	Clear the taxiway/runway	Taxi clear of the runway in use	Airport unsafe, do not land
Flashing white	Return to starting point on airport	Return to starting point on airport	Not applicable
Alternating red and green	Exercise extreme caution	Exercise extreme caution	Exercise extreme caution

uncontrolled airport. Other aircraft in or near the pattern might be tuned to the UNICOM frequency; everyone should be.

Even if the FBO is too busy to man his UNICOM (or has it turned off, for that matter), a transmission "in the blind" on the local UNICOM frequency, telling who you are, where you are, and what your intentions are, is good anti-collision insurance. Remember, most mid-airs and near-misses occur in clear weather in the vicinity of an airport.

When there is someone in the FBO office—and the UNICOM transceiver is operating—you may use it to obtain surface wind, perhaps an altimeter setting, types of fuel available, and the availability of ground transportation, food, and lodging. At a few unattended airports, keying your mike on the local UNICOM frequency will turn on runway lights. The codes used to do this are listed in the *Airman's Information Manual.*

MULTICOM. When operating at an airport where there isn't even a UNICOM available, use the MULTICOM frequency (122.9 MHz) to report your intentions. MULTICOM is normally reserved for air-to-air communications.

Aircraft operating to or from other nearby, uncontrolled airports may be making self-announce broadcasts on the same UNICOM or MULTICOM frequency. To help identify one airport from another, the airport name should be given at the beginning and end of each self-announce transmission (e.g., "Springdale Traffic, Cessna Skyhawk approaching downwind leg of pattern for landing on runway Three Eight, Springdale"). Because this is a traffic advisory for the benefit of other aircraft in the area, it makes more sense to identify your *type* of aircraft rather than give your registration number.

Chapter 7

The Examination

OBTAINING YOUR PILOT'S LICENSE will be an informal thing, as was your training. While learning, you attended ground school a couple of nights per week, or studied at home, to thoroughly absorb the subjects we've talked about here. You had appointments with your flight instructor several times a week for an hour's dual each time (most instructors will recommend that, for maximum effectiveness, you try to take no more than one hour of flight instruction per day), and you learned mostly by doing.

If you were an average student, there might have been a brief period—it usually comes after six or seven hours in the air—when you were discouraged because you couldn't seem to do anything right. But that was because you had learned enough by then to become critical of yourself; it was a good sign, not a bad one. Then, one morning after a few practice "touch-and-go" landings, your instructor told you to land and taxi back to the apron. There, without ceremony, he climbed out.

"Why don't you take 'er around alone? I'd like to stretch my legs for a while."

In a way, it was sort of anticlimatic. You had been flying the airplane for days, while he sat there apparently admiring the scenery and occasionally repeating one of his favorite phrases. Your solo wasn't much different than a dozen other flights you had recently made, except that the plane, relieved of the instructor's

175 pounds, seemed more eager than ever to get into the air.

After solo, you flew alone (except for a few hours dual cross-country and nighttime practice), but under the supervision of your instructor, accumulating the necessary flight time to qualify you for the private pilot flight test, or certification ride, as some call it.

With a minimum of 40 hours certified in your logbook, you may request, with your instructor's recommendation, that an FAA examiner administer your flight test (you must also have received a passing grade on the written test, which we'll come to momentarily). The flight test will be flown in an airplane with which you are familiar, in this case, our Cessna 150 trainer.

There's not much point in advising you not to be nervous; that's a very normal reaction. It might help you to keep in mind, however, that the examiner is a veteran pilot, a person dedicated to aviation, and he takes no pleasure in flunking anyone. Actually, he will be no more critical than your instructor (Fig. 7-1). So remember this: If you satisfied your instructor, you have nothing to fear from the examiner.

Fig. 7-1. The Flight Exam: There isn't much point in advising you not to be nervous; that's normal. Just remember, if you satisfied your instructor, you have nothing to fear from the FAA examiner.

THE FLIGHT TEST

The examiner will first grade you on your preflight check of the airplane. He will ask questions about the airplane's registration and airworthiness certificates, and he'll want to know if the airplane's maintenance schedule is current. He'll observe your radio technique and expect you to gather weather information and do a thorough job of planning a cross-country flight, with appropriate alternate airport and proper fuel reserves.

After takeoff, the examiner will observe your control technique and your respect for air traffic rules. He'll ask for climbing and gliding turns, stall recovery from climbing turns, and in other ways, make sure that you are a competent flying-machine operator. He will then request that you demonstrate your ability to maintain control of the airplane under simulated instrument conditions, and will usually put the plane in both climbing and descending turns (while you are wearing the instrument-flight hood) and expect you to return the plane to level flight.

He'll ask you to fly at least a portion of the previously plotted cross-country trip and, as we mentioned earlier, will probably require that you seek an alternate destination after you've shown aptitude on the original course.

The examiner will ordinarily ask to see more than one landing and will probably throw in a crosswind landing or two for good measure. But you have been doing all of these things for weeks and, again, if you satisfied your instructor, you have nothing to fear from the examiner.

There is one big difference between the examiner and your instructor. Don't look to the examiner for help or advice. He's there only to observe the level of your competence as a pilot. Don't try to flatter him, and above all don't try to *snow* him. He's heard all the artful dodges and excuses a thousand applicants could conjure. Just do everything the way you think it should be done, answer his questions, and if he asks something you can't answer, be honest about it.

One final and very important admonition: *Do not* make an appointment with an examiner unless you are sure you can keep it. The only acceptable excuse for cancelling your flight exam is bad weather (and that's a decision *you* should make, because he's interested in learning whether or not you're the kind who's inclined to push the weather). In short, the examiner is human, so I advise you to show him courtesy and consideration, if you expect it in return.

THE WRITTEN TEST

The written portion of the private pilot's exam is given periodically—the frequency being determined by the student-pilot population of a given area—by the FAA, usually in a post office or other federal building.

If you took a formal ground-school course, the FAA may come to your classroom to give the test. Or there might be an FAA-designated examiner already on staff at the ground school.

You must make a passing score on this test in order to be eligible for the flight exam mentioned above.

The test contains no "trick" questions, but because it is multiple choice, it could contain a few questions the correct answers to which are "more correct" than the other choices. As with all such tests, read each question carefully, and make sure that you understand the question before selecting the answer.

The examiner will expect you to bring a plotter and computer, but don't bother to bring notes. The test booklet will provide the aeronautical charts and mythical weather reports you'll need to plan the cross-country flight(s) called for in the exam.

The sample test that follows contains questions included in past FAA written tests. The questions here are limited to the subjects covered in this book. The official test you'll eventually take will not only cover additional subject areas, but will also contain questions for which you'll need to consult charts and graphs, and plot courses. Printing limitations prevent their inclusion here. (You would also need a plotter, computer, and further ground instruction to be able to answer those questions.)

If you can answer 42 of the following 60 questions correctly (70 percent), chances are, by the time you take the real thing, you'll do fine.

The *Private Pilot Question Book*, a complete, current list of possible test questions, is published periodically by the FAA and is available from commercial publishers and from the U.S. Government Printing Office, Washington, D.C.

****

Sample Written Test

1. Assume that the normal landing approach speed of your airplane is 75 MPH indicated airspeed at sea level. If you

plan to land at an airport where the elevation is 7,500 ft. MSL, the indicated approach speed should be

1— higher than at sea level and the true airspeed will be higher.
2— the same as at sea level and the true airspeed will be the same.
3— higher than at sea level, but the true airspeed will be the same.
4— the same as at sea level, but the true airspeed will be higher.

2. The *most* important rule to remember in the event of engine failure after becoming airborne, is to

1— quickly check the fuel supply for possible fuel exhaustion.
2— determine the wind direction to plan for your forced landing.
3— turn back immediately to the takeoff runway.
4— maintain a safe airspeed.

3. When taxiing with strong quartering tailwinds, which of the following aileron positions should be generally used?

1— Aileron PARALLEL to the ground on the side from which the wind is blowing.
2— Neutral (streamlined position).
3— Aileron UP on the side from which the wind is blowing.
4— Aileron DOWN on the side from which the wind is blowing.

4. In regard to the duration of Private Pilot Certificates, which statement is true?

1— They expire after a duration of 12 months.
2— They expire after a duration of 24 months.
3— They are issued without a specific expiration date.
4— When recency of experience requirements are not met the certificates expire.

5. To maintain the proper cruising altitude, if your airplane is not equipped with a radio, the altimeter should be set to

    1— the elevation of the airport of departure, or appropriate altimeter settings available prior to departure.

    2— the density altitude at the airport of departure.

    3— 29.92″ Hg at the airport of departure and whenever below 18,000 feet MSL.

    4— zero.

6. Unless otherwise authorized, two-way radio communications with ATC are required for landings or takeoffs

    1— at tower controlled airports within control zones only when weather conditions are less than VFR.

    2— at all tower controlled airports only when weather conditions are less than VFR.

    3— at all tower controlled airports regardless of the weather conditions.

    4— within control zones regardless of the weather conditions.

7. Select the true statement concerning wind circulation associated with pressure systems in the northern hemisphere, as shown on a Surface Weather Map.

    1— Wind circulates counterclockwise around high pressure areas and clockwise around low pressure areas.

    2— Wind circulates clockwise around high pressure areas and counterclockwise around low pressure areas.

    3— Wind circulates counterclockwise around both high pressure and low pressure areas.

    4— Wind circulates clockwise around both low pressure and high pressure areas.

8. Cumulonimbus clouds can best be described as

    1— thin, white, featherlike clouds in patches or narrow

bands formed on the crests of waves created by barriers in the windflow.

2— white or gray layers or patches of solid clouds, usually appearing in waves.

3— dense clouds, dark at lower levels extending many thousands of feet upward.

4— fluffy, white clouds appearing in layers and sometimes producing steady precipitation.

9. Which statement is true concerning In-Flight Weather Advisories?

1— AIRMETS will be issued concerning weather phenomena of such severity as tornadoes, embedded thunderstorms, squall lines, severe and extreme turbulence, ¼" hail, and severe icing.

2— SIGMETS include weather phenomena less severe than those covered by AIRMETS.

3— In-Flight Weather Advisories are also called PIREPS (Pilot Weather Reports).

4— In-flight advisories are unscheduled forecasts to advise en route aircraft of the development of potentially hazardous weather.

10. Hail is most likely to be associated with which type of cloud formation?

1— Cumulonimbus.

2— Cumulus.

3— Stratocumulus.

4— Cirrocumulus.

11. As you maneuver an airplane you should realize that it can be stalled

1— only when the nose is too high in relation to the horizon.

2— at any airspeed and in any flight attitude.

3— only when the airspeed decreases to the published stalling speed.

4— only when the nose is high and the airspeed is low.

12. What causes deviation errors in a magnetic compass?

   1— magnetic dip.
   2— acceleration and deceleration.
   3— the difference in location of true north and magnetic north.
   4— certain metals and electrical systems within the airplane.

13. The pitot system provides impact pressure for which instrument(s)?

   1— Airspeed indicator, vertical-speed indicator, and altimeter.
   2— Altimeter and vertical-speed indicator.
   3— Vertical-speed indicator.
   4— Airspeed indicator.

14. To counteract the effect of torque in a conventional single-engine propeller-driven airplane, a pilot should normally apply

   1— left rudder pressure during the takeoff roll and while climbing with full power.
   2— right rudder pressure when entering a glide from level cruising flight.
   3— right rudder pressure during the takeoff roll and while climbing with. full power.
   4— left rudder pressure when entering a climb from level cruising flight.

15. The temperature to which moist air must be cooled to become saturated is defined as

   1— sublimation.
   2— condensation nuclei.
   3— relative humidity.
   4— the dewpoint.

16. In all cases for an airplane to spin, it must first be

   1— partially stalled with one wing low and the throttle closed.

2— placed in a steep diving spiral.

3— stalled.

4— placed in a steep nose-high pitch attitude.

17. If an airplane is loaded 102 lbs. over maximum certificated gross weight, and gasoline is drained to bring the aircraft weight within limits, how much fuel should be drained?

1— 23 gallons.

2— 21 gallons.

3— 17 gallons.

4— 11 gallons.

18. A pilot planning a long distance flight from west to east in the conterminous United States would most likely find favorable winds associated with high and low pressure systems by planning to fly a course which is

1— south of both highs and lows.

2— north of a high.

3— north of a low.

4— south of a high.

19. Select the true statement concerning the use of flaps during the landing approach.

1— The use of flaps increases the airplane's controllability.

2— The use of flaps permits a decreased approach angle.

3— By using flaps, a steeper than normal angle of descent is possible without increasing the airspeed.

4— The use of flaps requires a higher indicated airspeed on the final approach.

20. When flying at a low altitude across a mountain range the greatest potential danger, caused by descending air currents, will usually be encountered on the

1— leeward side when flying into the wind.

2— windward side when flying into the wind.

3— leeward side when flying with the wind.

4— windward side when flying with the wind.

21. An airplane is usually affected by "ground effect" at what height above the surface?

    1— Between 100 and 200 feet above the surface in calm wind conditions.
    2— Less than half the airplane's wingspan above the surface.
    3— Twice the airplane's wingspan above the surface.
    4— Three to four times the airplane's wingspan.

22. Suppose that an airplane has been loaded in such a manner that the center of gravity is located aft of the CG limit. One characteristic that a pilot might experience with this airplane would be

    1— a longer takeoff run.
    2— the inability to recover from a stalled condition.
    3— stalling at higher than normal airspeed.
    4— the inability to flare during landings.

23. Filling the fuel tanks after the last flight of the day is a good operating procedure because this will

    1— force any existing water to the top of the tank away from the fuel lines to the engine.
    2— prevent expansion of the fuel by eliminating airspace in the tanks.
    3— prevent moisture condensation by eliminating airspace in the tanks.
    4— eliminate vaporization of the fuel.

24. You plan a flight of 95 statute miles and anticipate a groundspeed of 120 MPH. The airplane has 30 gallons usable fuel aboard, and the rate of fuel consumption is 8 gallons per hour. What would be the maximum flying time available with the remaining fuel when you arrive at your destination?

    1— 2 hours 57 minutes.
    2— 2 hours 40 minutes.
    3— 1 hour 38 minutes.
    4— 1 hour 15 minutes.

25. An airport control zone extends upward from the surface to the base of the

    1— Terminal Control Area.
    2— Positive Control Area.
    3— Continental Control Area.
    4— Airport Traffic Area.

26. The Continental Control Area for the 48 contiguous states consists of airspace

    1— at and above 14,500 feel MSL.
    2— at and below 14,500 feel MSL.
    3— within all restricted areas and prohibited areas.
    4— below 10,000 feet MSL.

27. Where are Airport Traffic Areas in effect?

    1— At all airports.
    2— Only at airports that have an operating control tower.
    3— Only at airports within a control zone.
    4— At all airports that have a Flight Service Station on the field.

28. Ground Control issues the following taxi instructions:

    "...CLEARED TO RUNWAY TWO ONE, WIND TWO ZERO ZERO AT ONE SIX, ALTIMETER TWO NINER EIGHT SEVEN, TIME ONE ONE FOUR THREE, TAXI NORTH ON THE RAMP. . ."

    From these instructions, you are cleared to taxi to

    1— and line up on Runway 21 and may take off unless instructed to hold by the tower.
    2— the north end of the ramp only.
    3— the runup area for Runway 21 only.
    4— and line up on Runway 21, but must receive permission for takeoff.

29. Suppose that you receive a flashing white light from a control tower during the runup prior to takeoff; what action should you take?

    1— None, since this light signal is applicable only to aircraft in flight.

2—Return to your starting point on the airport.

3—Taxi clear of the runway in use.

4—Proceed, exercising extreme caution.

30. To act as pilot in command of an aircraft, one must show by logbook endorsement the satisfactory (1) accomplishment of a flight review, or (2) completion of a pilot proficiency check within the preceding

    1—6 months.

    2—12 months.

    3—24 months.

    4—36 months.

31. The term "angle-of-attack" is best defined as the

    1—angle between the wing chord line and the direction of the relative wind.

    2—angle between the airplane's climb angle and the horizon.

    3—angle formed by the longitudinal axis of the airplane and the chord line of the wing.

    4—specific angle at which the ratio between lift and drag is the highest.

32. During operation *outside controlled airspace* at altitudes of more than 1,200 feet AGL, but less than 10,000 feet MSL, the minimum "horizontal distance from clouds" requirement for VFR flight is

    1—500 feet.

    2—1,000 feet.

    3—1,500 feet.

    4—2,000 feet.

33. GIVEN:

    Flight duration . . . . . . 50 minutes

    Rate of fuel consumption. . 10.7 GPH

    How much fuel would be used?

1— 8.9 gallons.
2— 8.5 gallons.
3— 8.3 gallons.
4— 9.2 gallons.

34. To comply with regulations, the selection of VFR cruising altitudes should be made on the basis of the magnetic

1— heading when more than 3,000 feet above the surface.
2— heading when more than 3,000 feet above sea level.
3— course when more than 3,000 feet above the surface.
4— course when more than 3,000 feet above sea level.

35. A (standard) preflight weather briefing would be incomplete if it did not include at least

1— synoptic weather and airspace restrictions.
2— forecast winds and weather and all pertinent radio navigation facilities.
3— winds aloft and current forecasts, weather synopsis (pressure systems and fronts), and possible hazardous weather.
4— the availability of Transcribed Weather Broadcasts (TWEBs) while en route, plus the items in response 2.

36. The basic VFR weather minimums for flights within controlled airspace below 10,000 feet MSL require the minimum visibility and distance under the clouds to be

1— 3 miles and 500 feet.
2— 1 mile and 500 feet.
3— 1 mile and clear of clouds.
4— 3 miles and 1,000 feet.

37. Suppose the following factors exist when determining VFR cruising altitudes for a flight where ground elevation is 1,500 feet MSL.

	True Course	Wind Correction Angle	Magnetic Variation
Leg I	183°	3° R	5° E
Leg II	185°	5° L	4° E

Select the altitudes that would comply with regulations for level cruising flight on Leg I and Leg II.

1— 7,500 feet MSL on Leg I; 8,500 feet MSL on Leg II.
2— 7,500 feet MSL on both legs.
3— 8,500 feet MSL on Leg I, 7,500 feet MSL on Leg II.
4— 8,500 feet MSL on both legs.

38. Regarding the characteristics and weather associated with a warm front, which of the following is a true statement?

1— The presence of thunderstorms in a warm front is usually easy to detect, since they are not embedded in cloud masses.
2— The frontal zone may have low ceilings and zero visibilities over a wide area.
3— Colder air is overtaking and replacing warmer air and this usually produces wide bands of precipitation ahead of the warm front surface position.
4— Squall lines sometimes develop 300 miles ahead of warm fronts.

39. Which of the following would decrease the stability of an air mass?

1— Warming from below.
2— Cooling from below.
3— Decrease in water vapor.
4— Sinking of the air mass.

40. When two aircraft are approaching each other head-on or nearly so, which aircraft should give way?

1— Regardless of the aircraft categories, a glider has the right-of-way over all engine-driven aircraft.

2— If the aircraft are of different categories, an airship
would have the right-of-way over a helicopter.

3— Regardless of the aircraft categories, the pilot of each
aircraft shall alter course to the right.

4— If the aircraft are of different categories, an airship
would have the right-of-way over an an airplane.

41. Approaching a VOR station while flying southwest at 8,500
feet MSL, you see a multiengine airplane at the same
altitude converging from your left, headed northwest toward the VOR. According to regulations which pilot should
give way and why?

1— You should give way since your airplane is slower
and more maneuverable than a multiengine airplane.

2— The pilot of the multiengine airplane should give way
since the airplane is not flying at a proper VFR
cruising altitude.

3— The multiengine airplane should give way since your
airplane is to its right and you have the right-of-way.

4— You should give way since the other airplane is to
your left and has the right-of-way.

42. Select the true statement regarding "ground effect."

1— Ground effect may cause an airplane to float on
landings or permit it to become airborne with
insufficient power to sustain flight outside of ground
effect.

2— Light single-engine airplanes usually encounter
"ground effect" at 200 or 300 feet above the surface.

3— In conditions of high gross weight, high density
altitude, and high temperature an airplane will
usually not encounter "ground effect."

4— Ground effect often causes an airplane to settle to
the surface immediately after becoming airborne.

43. Selected surface aviation weather reports

```
MLC  SA  1252  E23  OVC   7  126/34/30/3610/991
ADM  SA  1252  E20  BKN  20   37/26/3612G22/989
```

156

Which statement regarding the aviation weather reports above for McAlester (MLC) or Ardmore (ADM) is true?

1— At ADM the temperature/dewpoint spread is greater than at MLC.
2— At MLC the altimeter setting is 31.26 inches.
3— At ADM the 20,000-foot broken layer of clouds is more than 0.9 sky cover.
4— At ADM the temperature/dewpoint spread is such that the formation of fog is likely.

44. How should you establish contact with an En Route Flight Advisory Service station and what service would you normally expect?

1— Call "METRO" on 127.0 for routine weather, current reports on hazardous weather, and altimeter settings.
2— Call "FLIGHT WATCH" on 122.0 for information regarding routine weather and thunderstorm activity along your route.
3— Call "FLIGHT ASSISTANCE" on 122.5 for advisory service pertaining to severe weather.
4— Call "ARTCC" on assigned frequency and ask for Flight Watch services.

45. MDW SP — X M7 OVC 11/2R+F 990/63/61/3205/ 980/RF2 RB12

What is the visibility, weather, and obstruction to vision at MDW?

1— Visibility 11 miles, occasionally 2 miles, with rain + fog.
2— 11 miles visibility, except when rain + fog reduce it to 2 miles.
3— Visibility 1½ miles, heavy rain, and fog.
4— Visibility 1½ miles, rain, and heavy fog.

46. JFK SP W5 X 1/2F 180/68/64/1804/006/R04RVR 22V30 TWR VSBY1/4

Identify the wind conditions at JFK.

1— 360° at 6 knots
2— 180° at 4 knots
3— 040° at 22 variable to 30 knots
4— 040° at 18 knots

47. What causes surface winds to flow across the isobars at an angle rather than parallel to the isobars?

    1— Surface friction.
    2— Coriolis force.
    3— Heat radiation from the surface.
    4— The greater atmospheric pressure on the surface.

48. Which list of items makes up the useful load for an airplane?

    1— Pilot, passengers, usable fuel, oil, and baggage.
    2— Fuel on board, oil, passengers, and baggage.
    3— Pilot, passengers, baggage, and total fuel.
    4— Pilot, passengers, total fuel, oil, and cargo.

49. Determine the center of gravity of this airplane ready for takeoff on a VFR flight.

	Weight	Arm	MOM
Empty weight	3,351	79.3	265734
Oil	45	19.0	
Fuel	480	84.1	
Pilot and Copilot	340	85.3	
Passengers	340	121.2	
Baggage	51	153.0	

    1— 78.3″ aft of datum
    2— 81.1″ aft of datum
    3— 83.6″ aft of datum
    4— 85.3″ aft of datum

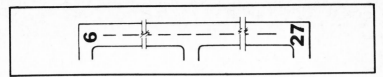

Fig. 7-2. Basic runway markings.

50. Refer to the runway direction markings in Fig. 7-2. The numbers 9 and 27 on the approach ends of the runway indicate that the runway is oriented approximately

   1— 090° and 270° magnetic.
   2— 009° and 027° true.
   3— 090° and 270° true.
   4— 009° and 027° magnetic.

51. Use Fig. 7-3. If an airplane weighs 3,400 lbs., what approximate weight would the airplane structure be supporting during a 60° banked turn while maintaining altitude?

   1— 8,400 lbs.
   2— 6,800 lbs.
   3— 4,400 lbs.
   4— 3,400 lbs.

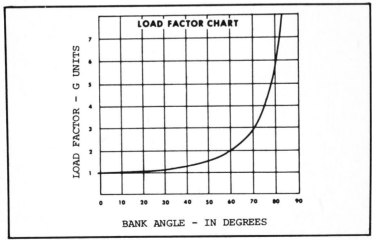

Fig. 7-3. Load factor chart.

52. Use Fig. 7-3. If the airplane has a maximum positive load factor of + 3.8 G units, the maximum bank in a level turn without exceeding this load factor would be

    1— unobtainable from the Load Factor Chart.
    2— approximately 82°
    3— approximately 74°
    4— approximately 67°

53. WINDS AND TEMPERATURES ALOFT FORECAST

FT	3000	6000	9000	12000
ATL	9900	2317+11	2423+07	2428+01

Refer to the Winds and Temperature Aloft Forecast above for Atlanta (ATL). The wind and temperature at 6,000 feet is forecast to be from

    1— 170° @ 23 knots; temperature 11° C.
    2— 230° @ 17 knots; temperature 11° C.
    3— 023° @ 11 knots; temperature 17° C.
    4— 170° @ 11 knots; temperature 17° C.

54. Refer to the airport symbols in Fig. 7-4. Select the true statement concerning these symbols.

    1— Symbol "H" depicts a Rotorcraft-Helicopter facility.
    2— Symbol "A" depicts an airport with emergency service or no service.
    3— Symbols "A", "C", "E", and "G" depict airports with services and fuel available.
    4— The stars on symbols "B", "E", and "G" indicate that these are military airports.

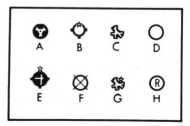

Fig. 7-4. Sectional chart airport symbols.

55. Assume that you desire to fly inbound to a VOR station on the 310 radial. The recommended procedure is to set the course selector to

1— 310° and make heading corrections away from the Course Deviation Indicator (CDI needle).
2— 310° and make heading corrections toward the Course Deviation Indicator (CDI needle).
3— 130° and make heading corrections toward the Course Deviation Indicator (CDI needle).
4— 130° and make heading corrections away from the Course Deviation Indicator (CDI needle).

56. Select the true statement concerning isobars and windflow patterns around high and low pressure systems that are shown on a Surface Weather Map.

1— When the isobars are far apart, crests of standing waves may be marked by stationary lenticular clouds.
2— Isobars connect contour lines of equal temperature.
3— When the isobars are close together, the pressure gradient force is greater and wind velocities are stronger.
4— Surface winds flow perpendicular to the isobars.

57. Which of the altimeters in Fig. 7-5 display an indicated altitude of more than 8,000 feet?

1— A, B, C, D.
2— B, E, F.
3— D, E.
4— A, B, F.

58. Refer to altimeter "B" in Fig. 7-5. Which one of the following indications is correct?

1— 7,880 feet.
2— 1,880 feet.
3— 8,880 feet.
4— 880 feet.

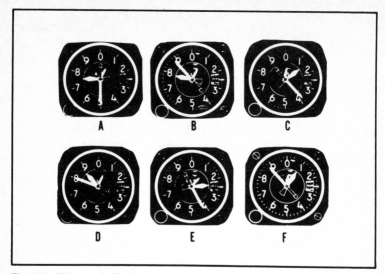

Fig. 7-5. Altimeter indications.

59. Which of the altimeters in Fig. 7-5 display an indicated altitude of less than 2,000 feet?

    1— D, E.
    2— C, F.
    3— B, E, F.
    4— A, C, E.

60. The weather condition normally associated with unstable air is

    1— good visibility, except in blowing sand or snow.
    2— stratiform clouds.
    3— fair to poor visibility.
    4— continuous precipitation.

ANSWERS

1. 4	21. 2	41. 3
2. 4	22. 2	42. 1
3. 4	23. 3	43. 1
4. 3	24. 1	44. 2
5. 1	25. 3	45. 3
6. 3	26. 1	46. 2
7. 2	27. 2	47. 1
8. 3	28. 3	48. 1
9. 4	29. 2	49. 3
10. 1	30. 3	50. 1
11. 2	31. 1	51. 2
12. 4	32. 4	52. 3
13. 4	33. 1	53. 2
14. 3	34. 3	54. 2
15. 4	35. 3	55. 3
16. 3	36. 1	56. 3
17. 3	37. 1	57. 3
18. 2	38. 2	58. 1
19. 3	39. 1	59. 2
20. 1	40. 3	60. 1

Glossary

ADF—Automatic direction finder.

aerodynamics—The forces, such as resistance, pressure, velocity and others involved in the movement of air or gases around a moving body, or the branch of dynamics and physics dealing with these forces.

AGL—Above ground level.

AIM—Airman's Information Manual. An FAA periodical providing basic flight information and air traffic control procedures.

ailerons—The primary control surfaces located at the trailing edges of the outer wing panels which, when moved up or down, cause the airplane in flight to bank.

airfoil—Any surface designed to create lift, either positive or negative, when moving through the air at a given speed. Examples include wings, control surfaces, propellers, and helicopter blades.

airspace—When used in aviation the term means the navigable sky, for all practical purposes, between ground level and 60,000 feet.

airspeed—The speed at which an aircraft is moving with relation to the air around it. It may be expressed as *indicated* airspeed, *calibrated* airspeed and *true* airspeed.

airspeed indicator—A flight instrument with a cockpit readout which, in terms of knots or mph, shows the difference between pitot pressure and static pressure. The reading obtained from the airspeed indicator is *indicated airspeed*.

alternator—An electrical device, serving the same purpose as the old-style generator, which is driven by the engine and supplies current to the battery and to all on-board electrical equipment except the ignition system.

altimeter—A flight instrument capable of displaying the height above sea level (or any other predetermined level), activated by an aneroid barometer measuring atmospheric pressure at the given altitude.

altimeter setting—The barometric-pressure reading in the small window provided for that purpose on the face of the altimeter.

angle of attack—The angle at which the chord line of the wing or any other airfoil meets the relative wind. It determines the amount of lift developed at a given airspeed.

approach—The maneuvers an airplane needs to perform prior to landing.

approach control—The ATC facility monitoring and directing traffic approaching an airport where such a facility is in operation.

ARSA—Airport Radar Service Area.

artificial horizon—A gyro instrument showing the attitude of the aircraft with reference to pitch and roll as compared to the horizon.

ATC—Air Traffic Control.

atmospheric pressure—The weight of the air surrounding the Earth. Standard atmospheric pressure is expressed as 29.92 inches of mercury or 1013.2 millibars.

avionics—A catch-all phrase for communication, navigation and related instrumentation in an aircraft. A contraction of *aviation electronics*.

back pressure—Aft force on the control wheel.

base leg—A part of the airport traffic pattern. A flight path at a right angle to the runway, following the downwind leg and followed by the final approach.

calibrated airspeed—Indicated airspeed corrected for instrument and installation errors.

carburetor heat—A heating unit located near the carburetor throat and controlled by a plunger in the cockpit. It is used to melt carburetor ice.

carburetor ice—Ice forming in the carburetor throat due to excessive moisture in the air.

compass, gyro—See *directional gyro*.

compass, magnetic—A compass which, during straight-and level-flight, automatically aligns itself with magnetic north.

constant-speed propeller—A controllable-pitch propeller which maintains a constant RPM by automatically changing the blade angle in relation to engine output.

course—The direction of flight of an aircraft across the ground.

course deviation indicator—The needle, bar, or other indicator which displays the position of an aircraft relative to a radial or bearing from or to a VOR.

cross-country flight—Flight during which a landing is made at a point other than the initial airport of takeoff, usually farther than 25 nautical miles.

dead-reckoning—A method of navigation by which an aircraft's course and time between two given points is estimated by taking into consideration course, speed, and wind components calculated with a wind triangle. The phrase is a bastardization of the term *deduced* reckoning.

density altitude—Pressure altitude corrected for prevailing temperature conditions.

dewpoint—The temperature to which air must cool without change in pressure or vapor content, in order for condensation to take place.

DG—Directional gyro.

directional gyro—A gyroscopic flight instrument which, when set to conform with the magnetic compass, will continue to indicate the aircraft heading for some time, regardless of turns or pitch changes. It tends to develop heading errors and must be adjusted intermittently.

downwind—Away from the direction from which the wind is blowing.

downwind leg—The flight path parallel to the runway in the direction opposite to landing. It is part of the standard airport traffic pattern.

drag—The force created by friction of the air on objects in motion. It must be overcome by thrust in order to achieve flight parallel to the relative wind. There are two types of drag, *induced* drag and *parasite* drag. Induced drag is created through the process of creating lift. Parasite drag is all drag from surfaces which do not contribute to lift. It increases with an increase in airspeed.

elevator—The primary control surface (attached to the horizontal stabilizer) which can be moved up or down to control the pitch of the aircraft. It is, in fact, a speed control as much as an altitude control.

E6-B—A circular-sliderule-type computer used to compute a variety of flight-related mathematics problems.

FAA—Federal Aviation Administration.

FAR—Federal Aviation Regulation.

FBO—Fixed-base operator.

final approach—The final portion of an airport traffic pattern during which the aircraft is aligned with the runway centerline.

fixed-base operator—A person or organization, at an airport, providing aviation services (e.g. flight instruction, fuel, maintenance).

fixed-pitch propeller—A propeller, the blade angle of which cannot be changed or adjusted.

FL—Flight level; FL180 stands for 18,000 feet.

flaps—Auxiliary control surfaces, usually located at the trailing edges of the inner wing panels, between the fuselage and the ailerons. Flaps can be extended and/or turned down to increase the wing camber and/or surface, creating additional lift and drag.

flare—A smooth leveling of the aircraft during which the nose is raised at the end of the glide and just prior to touchdown.

Flight Service Station—An FAA facility which provides weather briefings and other services to general aviation pilots, in person or by telephone or radio.

FPM—Feet per minute, in terms of rate of climb or descent

FSS—Flight Service Station.

generator—A device, identical in construction to an electrical motor which, when driven by the engine, generates electrical current and continuously recharges the battery.

Ground Control—An ATC service at controlled airports, responsible for the safe and efficient movement of aircraft and airport vehicles on the ground.

ground effect—Additional lift which takes effect when the aircraft is close to the ground. It is the result of air being compressed between the wings and the ground. Low-wing aircraft are more susceptible to the effect than are high-wing aircraft.

ground speed—The speed with which an aircraft moves relative to the surface of the Earth.

heading—The direction in which the aircraft flies through the air, not with reference to the ground. In other words, the direction in which the nose of the aircraft is pointing.

Hg—Mercury, as in 30.12″ Hg (inches of mercury).

horizontal stabilizer—The fixed horizontal portion of the tail section to which the elevator is attached.

HP—Horsepower.

IAS—Indicated airspeed.

IFR—Instrument flight rules, or weather conditions less than the minimum VFR requirements.

inches of mercury—Units of measurement of atmospheric pressure, used to indicate the height in inches to which a column of mercury will rise in a glass tube in response to the weight of the atmosphere exerting pressure on a bowl of mercury at the base of the tube.

indicated airspeed—The airspeed which is shown by the airspeed indicator. It is nearly always less than true airspeed, but usually not much different from calibrated airspeed.

induced drag—See *drag*.

kHz—Kilohertz or kilocycles.

knots—Nautical miles per hour.

kts.—Knots.

lift—The generally upward force created by the difference of pressure between the upper and lower surfaces of an airfoil in motion. In level flight it is balanced by the force of gravity.

magnetic course—The course of an aircraft referenced to magnetic north.

magnetic heading—The heading of an aircraft referenced to magnetic north.

magnetic north—The location, some distance from the geographic North Pole, where the Earth's magnetic lines converge.

magneto—A self-contained generator which supplies electrical current to the spark plugs in the ignition system.

manifold—An arrangement of tubing (on an aircraft engine) with one orifice on one end and several on the other.

MC—magnetic course.

manifold pressure—The pressure of the fuel-air mixture in the intake manifold.

MH—Magnetic heading.

MHz—Megahertz or megacycles.

millibar—A unit of atmospheric pressure. See *atmospheric pressure*.

mixture—The mixture of fuel and air necessary for combustion in reciprocating engines.

MPH—Statute miles per hour.

MSL—Mean sea level.

nautical mile—A unit of linear measure equal to 6076.1 feet.

needle and ball—An instrument which shows the rate of turn of the aircraft and displays whether the aircraft is in a skid or a slip. An older version of the turn-and-slip indicator and turn coordinator.

nm—Nautical mile(s).

parasite drag—See *drag*.

pattern—Airport landing pattern; the downwind and base legs and the final approach.

pilotage—Navigation by reference to visible landmarks. Used usually in conjunction with Sectional charts on which all meaningful landmarks are shown.

pilot in command—The pilot responsible for the operation and safety of an aircraft during flight time.

pitch—The attitude of the aircraft with reference to a horizontal axis at right angles to the fuselage. In other words, nose-down or nose-up.

pitot-static system—A device which compares impact pressure with static or atmospheric pressure and presents the result in the cockpit by means of the airspeed indicator, the altimeter, and the vertical-speed indicator.

pitot tube—A protrusion with a small orifice exposed to the airstream and designed to measure the pressure with which an aircraft meets the air. Also called a pitot head.

precession—The tendency of a directional gyro to gradually become unreliable due to friction.

propeller—A device consisting of two or more airfoil-shaped blades which is designed to convert the turning force of the engine into thrust.

PSI—Pressure in terms of pounds per square inch.

relative wind—The movement of air relative to the movement of an airfoil. It is parallel to and in the opposite direction of the flight path of an airplane.

RPM—Revolutions per minute.

rudder—The primary control surface attached to the vertical stabilizer, movement of which causes the tail of the aircraft to swing either left or right. It controls yaw.

runup—A pre-takeoff check of the performance of the engine and, in aircraft equipped with constant-speed props, the operation of the propeller.

Sectional chart—An aeronautical chart of a section of the U.S. at a scale of 1:500,000 or approximately 7 NM per inch.

service ceiling—The maximum altitude above sea level to which a particular aircraft can climb and then maintain horizontal flight under standard atmospheric conditions.

skid—Lateral movement of an airplane toward the outside of a turn, caused by incorrect use of the rudder.

slip—The tendency of an aircraft to lose altitude by slipping toward the center of a turn as a result of incorrect use of the rudder.

spin—A maneuver in which the airplane, after stalling, descends nearly vertically, nose-low, with the tail revolving around the vertical axis of the descent.

stall—The inability of an airplane to continue flight due to an excessive angle of attack. The airplane will either drop its nose and thus reduce the angle of attack and regain flying speed or, if forced to retain the excessive angle of attack, it may fall into a spin.

stall speed—The speed, at a given angle of attack, at which airflow separation begins and the stall occurs. Aircraft can stall at virtually any speed if an acceptable angle of attack is exceeded.

stall-spin—The combination of a stall followed by a spin, a major cause of fatal accidents.

stall warning—A device, usually involving a buzzer, a light or both, which indicates to the pilot that the aircraft is about to stall.

static vent—A hole, usually located in the side of the fuselage, which provides air at atmospheric pressure to operate the pitot-static system.

statute mile—A unit of measure equivalent to 5280 feet.

stick—Control wheel or yoke.

TAS—True airspeed.

taxi—To move an aircraft on the ground under its own power.

torque—The normal tendency of an aircraft to rotate to the left in reaction to the right-hand rotation of the propeller. It varies with changes in power.

tower—Control tower at a controlled airport.

trim tab—A small airfoil attached to a control surface, usually the elevator and occasionally the rudder, which can be adjusted to cause changes in the position of the control surface under varying flight conditions.

true airspeed—The actual speed at which an aircraft is moving in relation to undisturbed air. It is calibrated airspeed adjusted for actual air density and altitude.

true course—Course referenced to true north.

true heading—Heading referenced to true north.

true north—Geographic (not magnetic) north. The direction to the northern end of the Earth's axis.

turn-and-slip indicator—See *needle and ball.*

UNICOM—Aeronautical advisory station for communication with aircraft. UNICOMs are usually manned by FBOs or airport personnel and provide pilots with such information as the active runway, wind direction and velocity, and other conditions of importance to pilots. UNICOMs are not authorized to give takeoff or landing clearances, or in any way control traffic (except when relaying word from ATC, in which case any such transmission must be preceded by *ATC clears . . .*).

unusual attitude—Any attitude of an aircraft in terms of pitch or roll or both which is beyond the normal operating attitude. Recovery from unusual attitudes by reference to instruments is an important part of instrument training.

vertical-speed indicator—An instrument, part of the pitot-static system, which indicates the rate of climb or descent in terms of FPM. It is usually calibrated in units of either 100 or 1000 FPM.

vertical stabilizer—A fixed vertical airfoil on the empennage to which the rudder is attached.

VFR—Visual flight rules, or weather conditions equal to or better than minimum visual flight rule requirements.

VHF—Very high frequency; electromagnetic frequencies between 30 and 300 MHz.

VOR—Very high frequency omni-directional radio range; a ground-based VHF navigation aid.

VSI—Vertical-speed indicator.

WCA—Wind correction angle.

wind shear—An abrupt change in wind direction or velocity.

yaw—The movement of an aircraft to either side, turning around its vertical axis, without banking.

yoke—Control wheel; stick.

Index

Edited by Carl H. Silverman